HEALTHY VEG RECIPE

BY <u>BRYAN RYLEE</u>

Introduction 5

Introduction

I WANT TO THANK YOU AND CONGRATULATE YOU ON CHOOSING THE BOOK, "HEALTHY VEGAN GREEK RECIPES".
THE MERE FACT THAT YOU ARE READING THIS BOOK MEANS YOU HAVE MADE A DECISION THAT WILL CHANGE YOUR LIFESTYLE – A CHANGE THAT WILL MAKE YOU HEALTHIER AND HAPPIER. YOU MUST HAVE READ A HUNDRED TIMES THAT HEALTHY EATING HABITS HAVE A POSITIVE EFFECT, NOT ONLY ON YOUR WEIGHT AND HEALTH, BUT ALSO YOUR OPTIMISTIC ATTITUDE TO WHATEVER IS HAPPENING AROUND. AND THIS BOOK IS NOT AN EXCEPTION. IT WILL GUIDE YOU THROUGH THE PROCESS OF PREPARING HEALTHY AND TASTY GREEK VEGAN DISHES WITH INGREDIENTS THAT ARE EASY TO FIND AND COOK. YOU WILL FIND A WIDE RANGE OF RECIPES, WHICH CAN BE ADAPTED FOR A HEALTHY BREAKFAST AND A HEARTY LUNCH, AND SOME THAT WILL GO WELL AS A DINNER OR A LIGHT SUPPER. WE HAVE INCLUDED A LARGE ASSORTMENT OF DELICIOUS DESSERTS AND SNACKS. THE RECIPES PROVIDE A STEP-BY-STEP DESCRIPTION OF HOW TO COOK HEALTHY AND, AT THE SAME TIME, TASTY FOOD, INCLUDING SOUPS AND STEWS MADE OF LEGUMES, VEGETABLES AND GREENS.

THE SELECTION OF GREEK VEGAN CUISINE RECIPES IS INITIALLY CONDITIONED WITH A LARGE VARIETY OF VEGETABLES AND HERBS, GRAINS, WINE, FISH AND OTHER INGREDIENTS. AS IN EVERY SIMILAR CUISINE, OLIVE OIL IS ONE OF THE KEY ELEMENTS OF GREEK FOODS. IT IS SIMPLY AN OUTSTANDING REFLECTION OF TRADITIONAL MEDITERRANEAN CUISINE CONTAINING A HIGH LEVEL OF NUTRIENTS AND A LOW AMOUNT OF ANIMAL FATS. THE POPULARITY OF GREEK CUISINE,

PARTICULARLY VEGAN CUISINE, HAS TO DO WITH ITS HISTORY, GEOGRAPHY AND CLIMATE ALLOWING THE ABILITY TO CULTIVATE DIFFERENT TYPES OF FRUITS, VEGETABLES AND GRAINS. ALTHOUGH GREEK CUISINE HAD BEEN AFFECTED BY ROMAN, BYZANTIUM, TURKISH AND OTHER CULTURES, IT HAS STILL PRESERVED ITS UNIQUENESS.

AS MENTIONED, OLIVE OIL PLAYS A MAIN ROLE IN GREEK VEGAN CUISINE, IT IS PRESENT IN MANY DISHES. VEGETABLES ALSO PLAY AN IMPORTANT ROLE IN THE CUISINE, THE MAIN VEGETABLES INCLUDE TOMATOES, EGGPLANT, GREEN BEANS, GREEN PEPPER, ONIONS AND OKRA. GREEK COOKING OFTEN CALLS FOR STUFFING VEGETABLES. THE MOST FAMOUS DISH IS *TOMATES GEMISTA*, STUFFED TOMATOES WITH RICE, ONIONS, HERBS AND MEAT. GREECE HAS A HUGE VARIETY OF APPETIZERS AND SALADS MADE FROM FRESH VEGETABLES AND FRUIT. ANYONE WHO HAS VISITED GREECE AT LEAST ONCE MUST HAVE TRIED THE FAMOUS GREEK SALAD WHICH IS MADE FROM FRESH RIPE RED TOMATOES, ONIONS, CUCUMBERS, GREEN PEPPERS, OLIVES, OLIVE OIL, FETA CHEESE (IF NOT VEGAN) AND OREGANO. WITH SO MANY KINDS OF VEGETABLES GREECE IS A REAL PARADISE FOR PEOPLE FOLLOWING THE VEGAN DIET.

GREECE IS ALSO WELL KNOWN FOR ITS VARIOUS HERBS AND SPICES, SO IT IS NOT SURPRISING THAT GREEK MEALS ARE SO TASTY AND FLAVORFUL. HERBS AND SPICES CAN BE USED FLAKED OR WHOLE, FRESH OR DRIED, AS LEAVES OR STEMS, AS SEEDS, AND IN OTHER VARIATIONS. THE MOST POPULAR AMONG THESE ARE OREGANO, MINT, GARLIC, ONION, DILL AND BAY LAUREL LEAVES.

FRUITS ARE ALSO AN IMPORTANT STAPLE IN THE GREEK DIET. TYPICALLY, A BOWL OF FRESH FRUIT IS

SERVED WITH ALMOST EVERY MEAL. YOU CAN EAT EITHER FRESH OR DRIED FRUITS, SUCH AS PLUMS, APRICOTS, APPLES, GRAPES, FIGS, DATES, AND CHERRIES. GREEK COOKING ALSO HAS THE TRADITION OF BAKING OR ROASTING FRUITS IN THE OVEN. IN THIS BOOK YOU CAN FIND SOME WONDERFUL RECIPES INCORPORATING BAKED FRUIT.

THE OTHER CONSISTENT INGREDIENT OF THE GREEK VEGAN CUISINE IS WHEAT. THIS IS A NATIONAL STAPLE PRODUCT, ONE THAT IS FOUND IN MANY RECIPES, AND IT HAS BEEN CULTIVATED IN GREECE FOR THOUSANDS OF YEARS. IT'S USED IN THE PREPARATION OF DIFFERENT TYPES OF FOODS, SUCH AS BREAD, NAMELY IN THE WELL KNOWN PITA BREAD. BULGUR, MADE OF CRACKED WHOLE WHEAT, CAN BE EATEN SEPARATELY OR ADDED INTO SOUPS OR SALADS.

THE FINAL TYPICAL GRAIN FOOD OF GREEK VEGAN COOKING IS RICE. THIS IS USED IN PILAFS AND BAKES, SERVED WITH STEWS, OR WRAPPED IN GRAPE LEAVES TO MAKE DOLMADES.

The Greek Vegan Cuisine – Most Common Ingredients

THE OLIVE - OLIVES ARE USED IN COOKING IN MANY COUNTRIES, BUT THE MOST POPULAR OLIVE IN THE WORLD ARE THE ALMOND SIZED BLACK OLIVES, KALAMATA, WHICH HAVE A RICH AND FRUITY TASTE. THE COLOR OF THE OLIVES DEPENDS ON THE SEASON DURING WHICH THEY WERE CROPPED. IN GREECE YOU CAN OFTEN FIND OLIVES STUFFED WITH GARLIC, WILD FENNEL, LEMON OR HOT PEPPER FLAKES. IN GREECE OLIVES ARE ALSO EATEN WHOLE. KALAMATA AND OTHER DARK OLIVES ARE STORED EITHER IN VINEGAR OR IN OLIVE OIL. OLIVES PROVIDE AN EXCELLENT AND IMPRESSIVE TANG TO MANY DISHES, FROM VEGETABLE SALADS TO MEAT SAUCES.

OLIVE OIL - ONE CANNOT IMAGINE GREEK CUISINE WITHOUT OLIVE OIL. IT IS RICH IN MINERALS AND VITAMINS. GREEK OLIVE OIL, MAINLY THE EXTRA VIRGIN OIL, IS IN GREAT DEMAND AS GREEK PEOPLE MAKE THE WORLD'S BEST OLIVE OIL. EXTRA VIRGIN OIL IS OBTAINED IN THE PROCESS OF FIRST PRESSING OF THE OLIVES; IT IS UNREFINED AND HAS A MILDER AND A MORE DELICATE TASTE. IN GREEK CUISINE OLIVE OIL IS THE MAIN COOKING FAT. IT IS USED IN COOKING OF SOUPS AND STEWS, FOR FLAVORING SALADS, AND EVEN IN BAKING.

BEANS AND LEGUMES - BEANS AND LEGUMES ARE AN IMPORTANT PART OF GREEK COOKING. BEANS ARE A GOOD SOURCE OF FIBER AND PROTEINS, AND THEY ALSO HELP TO LOWER CHOLESTEROL LEVEL IN BLOOD. BEANS ARE ALSO A PERFECT FOOD FOR PEOPLE TRYING TO LOSE WEIGHT, AS EATING SMALL PORTIONS

9

KEEPS YOU FULL FOR A LONG TIME. ALONG WITH OTHER LEGUMES, SUCH AS LENTILS, CHICKPEAS AND SPLIT PEAS, BEANS ARE USED IN SOUPS AND SALADS, AS WELL AS IN STEWED, ROASTED MEALS AND PATTIES.

LEMON - THIS IS WIDELY USED IN GREEK COOKING AND IS ONE OF THE DEFINING FLAVORS. GREEKS USE LEMON JUICE IN ALMOST EVERY DISH. THEY SQUEEZE FRESH LEMON OVER BEAN SALADS, GRILLED MEATS, GRILLED CHICKEN KEBABS AND GREEN SALADS. LEMON ZEST AND JUICES ARE ALSO A DELICIOUS ADDITION TO SWEETS AND DESSERTS, PROVIDING A PLEASANT SAVORY TASTE.

CINNAMON - THIS IS A VERY POPULAR SPICE IN GREECE. GREEK PEOPLE USE CINNAMON IN PREPARING CAKES, COOKIES AND CANDIES, AS WELL AS WHEN MARINATING MEAT AND FISH. THIS SPICE ADDS A UNIQUE TASTE TO ANY FOOD.

OREGANO - THIS IS THE MOST WIDELY USED HERB IN THE GREEK CUISINE. IT IS MOSTLY USED WITH MEAT, SALADS (ESPECIALLY IN THE FAMOUS GREEK SALAD), IN TOMATO SAUCES, FISH AND EGG DISHES,AND WITH CHEESE, AS WELL AS WITH VARIOUS VEGETABLES AND LEGUMES. IN GREECE YOU MAY COME ACROSS OREGANO ON THE TABLE TOGETHER WITH SALT AND PEPPER. DRINKING OREGANO TEA IS RECOMMENDED AGAINST COUGHS AND INDIGESTION.

WILD GREENS - WILD GREENS ARE VERY POPULAR IN THE GREEK CUISINE. THEY ARE USED RAW, BOILED AND BAKED IN CASSEROLES. THEY ARE USUALLY SERVED SPRINKLED WITH LEMON JUICE AND OLIVE OIL. WILD GREENS ARE RICH IN VITAMINS AND MINERALS, AS WELL AS ALSO BEING HIGH IN ANTI-OXIDANTS. ONE OF THE MOST COMMON GREENS IN GREEK COOKING IS SPINACH, THIS IS USED BOTH FRESH AND FROZEN. WHEN RAW, SPINACH HAS A MUCH MILDER TASTE THAN AFTER IT HAD BEEN COOKED.

GREEN HERBS - HERBS ARE A KEY INGREDIENT IN THE GREEK CUISINE, AND HAVE BEEN USED IN GREECE FROM ANCIENT TIMES. CILANTRO, PARSLEY, MINT, AND GREEN DILL ARE THE MAIN GREEN HERBS USED IN COOKING. THEY PROVIDE A FRESH AND UNIQUE FLAVOR TO ANY DISH. THEY ARE ALSO GREAT SOURCES OF VITAMINS AND ANTIOXIDANTS.

Appetizers
Corn and Garbanzo Bean Patties
(Vegan)

THESE FANTASTIC PATTIES CAN BE SERVED WITH ANY
MAIN COURSE. THEY ARE VERY TASTY AND AROMATIC.
THE BEANS PROVIDE A HIGH PROTEIN CONTENT, SO
THIS DISH CAN BE EASILY INTEGRATED INTO YOUR
HEALTHY DIET.
PREPARATION TIME 2 MINUTES
COOKING TIME 8 MINUTES
SERVES: 6

INGREDIENTS:
1 TSP CANOLA OIL
1 TBSP CANOLA OIL
1½ CUPS FRESH OR FROZEN CORN KERNELS (THAWED)
2 TBSP SHALLOTS, CHOPPED
½ TSP GREEK OREGANO

2 TSP FRESH ITALIAN PARSLEY, MINCED
1 19OZ (230G) CAN GARBANZO BEANS, DRAINED
1 CUP FRESH BREADCRUMBS
2 TBSP FINE GRAIN CORNMEAL, OR 2 TABLESPOONS
MASA HARINA
½ TSP SALT
2 TBSP RED BELL PEPPERS, MINCED
1 TBSP POLENTA (COARSE CORNMEAL)

DRESSING
¼ CUP FRESH LEMON JUICE
⅓ CUP EXTRA VIRGIN OLIVE OIL
SALT, TO TASTE
FRESH GROUND BLACK PEPPER, TO TASTE

GARNISH
5OZ (150G) ARUGULA LEAVES OR MIXED GREENS
(RINSED, DRAINED)
FRESH GARLIC CHIVES, MINCED

DIRECTIONS:
1.   ADD 1 TEASPOON OF OLIVE OIL TO A LARGE SKILLET AND SET OVER A MEDIUM-HIGH HEAT. STIR IN THE SHALLOTS, CORN AND OREGANO, AND COOK FOR A COUPLE OF MINUTES. REMOVE FROM THE HEAT AND LET IT COOL. ADD THE FRESH PARSLEY AND STIR TO COMBINE.
2.   PLACE THE CORNMEAL, GARBANZO BEANS, 2 TABLESPOONS OF THE RESERVED GARBANZO BEAN LIQUID, BREAD CRUMBS, MINCED RED BELL PEPPER AND SALT INTO A BLENDER. PROCESS UNTIL COARSELY GROUND.
3.   ADD THE FRIED CORN AND SHALLOT MIXTURE TO THE BLENDED MIXTURE, AND ADD ANOTHER TABLESPOON OF THE BEAN LIQUID AND BLEND (8-10 TIMES) UNTIL FINELY GROUND.
4.   MOISTEN YOUR HANDS AND SHAPE THE MIXTURE INTO 6 PATTIES. GENTLY COAT THE PATTIES WITH POLENTA AND FRY IN THE REMAINING TABLESPOON OF OLIVE OIL OVER A MEDIUM TO HIGH HEAT. COOK THE PATTIES IN BATCHES, 3 AT A TIME. LET THEM COOK FOR 3-4 MINUTES PER SIDE, THEN TURN TO BROWN ON THE OTHER SIDE.
5.   PLACE THE DONE PATTIES IN THE OVEN AT

14

200°F (100°C) TO KEEP WARM. MAKE THE DRESSING BY
COMBINING THE FRESH LEMON JUICE, OLIVE OIL,
SALT AND PEPPER IN A SMALL CUP.
DRIZZLE THE MIXTURE OVER THE ARUGULA (OR
MIXED GREENS) AND LIGHTLY TOSS TO COAT.
DIVIDE THE HERBS AMONG SIX SERVING BOWLS AND
TOP WITH THE COOKED PATTIES. DECORATE WITH
FRESH CHIVES AND SERVE IMMEDIATELY WITH THE
REMAINING DRESSING.

VEGAN MOUSSAKA

PREPARATION TIME 30 MINUTES
COOKING TIME 2 HOURS
SERVES: 12

INGREDIENTS:
5 LARGE RUSSET POTATOES, PEELED AND CUT INTO
CHUNKS (3½LBS)
4 CLOVES GARLIC, PEELED
¼ CUP, PLUS 2 TBSP OLIVE OIL, DIVIDED
1 LARGE ONION, CHOPPED (1½ CUPS)
3 TBSP DRIED OREGANO
2 15OZ (430G) CANS CHOPPED TOMATOES
⅔ CUP GREEN LENTILS
1 BAY LEAF
1 CINNAMON STICK
2 MEDIUM EGGPLANTS, SLICED
2 SMALL ZUCCHINI, SLICED
3 TOMATOES, THINLY SLICED
SALT, TO TASTE
GROUND BLACK PEPPER, TO TASTE

DIRECTIONS:
1.   PLACE THE PEELED POTATOES AND GARLIC
IN A LARGE POT OF BOILING SALTED WATER
AND COOK FOR 10 MINUTES, OR UNTIL TENDER.
DRAIN, RESERVING THE COOKING LIQUID.
2.   MASH THE POTATOES AND GARLIC, ADDING
¼ CUP OLIVE OIL AND 2 CUPS OF THE RESERVED
LIQUID. SEASON THE PUREE WITH SALT AND
PEPPER.
3.   ADD 2 TABLESPOONS OF OLIVE OIL TO A
LARGE GRIDDLE AND SET OVER A MODERATE
HEAT.
4.   STIR IN THE ONION AND OREGANO, AND
SAUTÉ FOR 4-5 MINUTES, UNTIL GOLDEN AND
TRANSLUCENT.

16

5.   STIR IN THE LENTILS, TOMATOES, CINNAMON STICK AND BAY LEAF, AND POUR IN 3 CUPS OF THE RESERVED POTATO COOKING LIQUID. REDUCE THE HEAT AND SIMMER, COVERED, FOR ABOUT 40 MINUTES UNTIL THE LENTILS HAVE SOFTENED.

6.   DISCARD THE CINNAMON STICK AND BAY LEAF. TRANSFER THE LENTIL MIXTURE TO A FOOD PROCESSOR AND PULSE UNTIL CHUNKY. SEASON THE PUREE WITH SALT AND PEPPER.

7.   LINE A BAKING DISH WITH A PAPER TOWEL. ARRANGE THE EGGPLANT SLICES ON IT, SEASON WITH SALT AND LET IT SIT FOR 25-30 MINUTES. THEN SLIGHTLY RINSE AND DRAIN.

8.   PREHEAT OVEN TO 350°F (170°C). OIL A DEEP BAKING DISH WITH COOKING SPRAY.

9.   PLACE 1½ CUPS OF THE LENTIL MIXTURE INTO THE PREPARED DISH. IN AN EVEN LAYER ARRANGE THE EGGPLANT SLICES, ZUCCHINI AND TOP WITH TOMATOES. ADD A FURTHER 2 CUPS OF THE LENTIL MIXTURE ON TOP. TOP WITH HALF OF THE MASHED POTATOES, THEN PLACE THE REMAINING EGGPLANT SLICES, LAID OVER BY THE REMAINING LENTIL MIXTURE.

10.   FINALLY, TOP WITH THE REMAINING POTATOES AND BAKE IN THE OVEN FOR 1½ HOURS, OR UNTIL GOLDEN BROWN.

Greek Style Hummus

TRADITIONAL HUMMUS IS A TASTY CHICKPEA DIP THAT IS WELL KNOWN IN GREECE, AS WELL AS ALL OVER THE WORLD. THIS IS A QUICK AND SIMPLE RECIPE OF GREEK-STYLE HUMMUS. ALTHOUGH THIS RECIPE CALLS FOR GARBANZO BEANS, TAHINI, LEMON AND GARLIC AS THE MAIN INGREDIENTS, YOU CAN ALSO ADD RED PEPPER FLAKES, BELL PEPPERS AND PINE NUTS. ENJOY WITH CRISPY PITA BREAD.

PREPARATION TIMES 10 MINUTES
COOKING TIME 0 MINUTES
SERVES: 2-4

INGREDIENTS:
1-2 CLOVES GARLIC, PRESSED

18

19 OZ (530G) CAN GARBANZO BEANS (RESERVE SOME LIQUID)
4 TBSP LEMON JUICE
2 TBSP TAHINI
1 TSP SALT
2 TBSP OLIVE OIL
GROUND BLACK PEPPER, TO TASTE

DIRECTIONS:

1. PLACE THE GARBANZO BEANS (INCLUDING GARBANZO LIQUID), TAHINI, GARLIC, OLIVE OIL, LEMON JUICE, SALT AND GROUND BLACK PEPPER IN A BLENDER AND PROCESS UNTIL SMOOTH. IF YOU GET A VERY THICK MIXTURE, ADD MORE BEAN LIQUID.

2. PLACE THE HUMMUS IN A SERVING BOWL, OR ADD TO THE SIDE OF A DINNER PLATE, DRIZZLE WITH A LITTLE OLIVE OIL AND SERVE.

Eggplant Purée with Walnuts

THE COMBINATION OF EGGPLANT AND SPINACH IS DELICIOUS. THIS HEALTHY DISH CAN BE SERVED EITHER AS A SIDE DISH OR AS A MAIN COURSE.

PREPARATION TIME10 MINUTES
COOKING TIME 25 MINUTES
SERVES: 2

INGREDIENTS:
2 LARGE EGGPLANTS
2 - 4 GARLIC CLOVES, PEELED AND MINCED
½ CUP SHELLED WALNUTS, COARSELY CHOPPED
½ CUP EXTRA-VIRGIN OLIVE OIL
2 TBSP STRAINED FRESH LEMON JUICE
1 - 2 TBSP RED WINE VINEGAR
SALT, TO TASTE
½ -1 TSP SUGAR (OPTIONAL)

DIRECTIONS:
1.   PREHEAT OVEN TO 450°F (220°C).
2.   THOROUGHLY WASH THE EGGPLANTS AND DRAIN. USING A FORK, PIERCE THE EGGPLANTS IN SEVERAL PLACES.
3.   PLACE THE EGGPLANTS ON AN UNGREASED BAKING DISH AND PLACE IN THE OVEN. BAKE FOR 20- 25 MINUTES, TURNING 1-2 TIMES, UNTIL THE SKIN IS SHRIVELED. WITHDRAW FROM THE OVEN AND LET THEM COOL FOR 5 MINUTES.
4.   MEANWHILE, PLACE THE WALNUTS, GARLIC AND 2 TABLESPOONS OF THE OLIVE OIL IN A BLENDER AND PROCESS UNTIL THE MIXTURE RESEMBLES A PASTE.
5.   REMOVE THE STEMS AND HALVE THE EGGPLANTS LENGTHWISE. SCRAPE OUT THE PULP WITH A SPOON, REMOVING THE SEEDS.

PLACE THE EGGPLANT IN A BLENDER AND PULSE FOR A SHORT TIME.

6.   ADD THE VINEGAR, LEMON JUICE AND REMAINING OLIVE OIL, AND PROCESS UNTIL WELL BLENDED. SEASON WITH SALT TO TASTE, AND ENJOY. YOU MAY ADD A SMALL AMOUNT OF SUGAR AS EGGPLANTS CAN SOMETIMES HAVE A TRACE OF BITTERNESS.

GREEK FAVA

FAVA IS AN AUTHENTIC GREEK DISH MADE OF SPLIT
PEAS. IT MAKES A PERFECT SIDE DISH OR APPETIZER.

PREPARATION TIMES 0 MINUTES
COOKING TIME 1 HOUR
SERVES: 4 - 6

INGREDIENTS:
1 CUP OF SANTORINI FAVA (OR YELLOW SPLIT PEAS)
1 MEDIUM-LARGE RED ONION, CHOPPED
2 TBSP OLIVE OIL
½ TSP SEA SALT

GARNISH
EXTRA VIRGIN OLIVE OIL
FRESHLY SQUEEZED LEMON JUICE
THINLY SLICED SPRING ONIONS
CAPERS

DIRECTIONS:
1. THOROUGHLY WASH THE FAVA AND PLACE IN A LARGE SAUCEPAN.
2. POUR IN ENOUGH WATER TO COVER, AND BRING TO A BOIL OVER MEDIUM-HIGH HEAT. WHEN A FROTH FORMS ON THE SURFACE OF THE WATER, POUR OFF THE WATER, RINSE THE FAVA AND RETURN BACK TO THE SAUCEPAN, ADDING 2½ CUPS OF WATER.
3. BRING THE WATER BACK TO THE BOIL. ONCE IT BEGINS TO BOIL, SLOW DOWN THE HEAT AND LET IT SIMMER FOR 40-50 MINUTES. YOU MAY NEED TO ADD MORE WATER IF YOU SEE THAT THE FAVA BEGINS TO DRY OUT. WHEN THE FAVA IS TENDER, REMOVE FROM THE HEAT AND LET THEM COOL.
4. PLACE THE FAVA IN A FOOD PROCESSOR OR BLENDER, AND PULSE UNTIL SMOOTH AND

CREAMY.
5.   LADLE THE DISH INTO SMALL PLATES,
DRIZZLE WITH LEMON JUICE AND OLIVE OIL,
AND GARNISH WITH CHOPPED SPRING ONIONS
AND CAPERS BEFORE SERVING.

Briam (Greek potato and zucchini bake)

BRIAM IS A TRADITIONAL GREEK POTATO-BASED BAKE,
FLAVORED WITH OLIVE OIL AND FRESH PARSLEY.
WARM OR COOL IT IS ABSOLUTELY DELICIOUS.

PREPARATION TIME 15 MINUTES
COOKING TIME 1 HR 30 MINUTES
SERVES: 4

INGREDIENTS;
2.2.2 LBS. (1KG) POTATOES, PEELED AND SLICED INTO
ROUNDS
4 LARGE ZUCCHINIS, SLICED INTO ROUNDS
4 MEDIUM RED ONIONS, SLICED INTO ROUNDS
½ CUP (125ML) OLIVE OIL
6 FRESH PLUM TOMATOES, PUREED
2 TABLESPOONS FRESH PARSLEY, CHOPPED
SEA SALT, TO TASTE
GROUND BLACK PEPPER, TO TASTE

DIRECTIONS:

1. PREHEAT THE OVEN TO 390°F (200°C).
2. PLACE THE ZUCCHINI ROUNDS, POTATOES ROUNDS AND RED ONIONS IN A LARGE RIMMED BAKING DISH. TOP WITH THE PUREED TOMATOES, DRIZZLE WITH OLIVE OIL, AND SEASON WITH SALT, FRESHLY GROUND PEPPER AND PARSLEY.
3. GENTLY MIX THE VEGETABLES TO COAT EVENLY. ADD ABOUT ½ CUP OF WATER TO THE DISH AND TRANSFER TO THE OVEN.
4. BAKE THE MIXTURE FOR 90 MINUTES; STIRRING OCCASIONALLY AND ALSO ADDING A LITTLE MORE WATER IF NECESSARY TO PREVENT FROM STICKING TO THE BOTTOM. REMOVE THE DISH FROM THE OVEN, TASTE AND ADJUST WITH SEASONING IF NEEDED. LET IT STAND FOR 10 MINUTES TO COOL BEFORE SERVING.

Rice-Stuffed Tomatoes

THIS WONDERFUL RECIPE WAS PROVIDED BY A FRIEND
FROM GREECE. THESE STUFFED TOMATOES ARE
WONDERFUL HOT OR COOL. YOU CAN ENJOY THIS DISH
WITH A POTATO SALAD AND SALAD GREENS.

PREPARATION TIME 15 MINUTES
COOKING TIME 55 MINUTES
SERVES: 6

INGREDIENTS:
1 BAY LEAF
1 TSP OLIVE OIL
1 CUP WHITE RICE
1-1½ CUPS VEGETABLE STOCK
1¼ CUPS WHITE WINE
6 MEDIUM TOMATOES
¼ CUP GREEN ONIONS, CHOPPED
¼ CUP FRESH BASIL LEAVES, CHOPPED

DIRECTIONS:
1. CUT A SMALL SLICE OFF THE TOPS OF THE TOMATOES AND SET ASIDE.
2. GENTLY DISCARD THE SEEDS WITH A TEASPOON. THINLY CHOP THE PULP AND PLACE IN A POT. PUT THE HOLLOWED TOMATOES, CUT SIDE DOWN, IN A BAKING DISH.
3. ADD THE RICE TO THE POT AND COOK FOR A MINUTE OVER A MEDIUM-HIGH HEAT.
4. POUR IN ¼ CUP OF THE WINE, THE VEGETABLE STOCK, OLIVE OIL AND THE BAY LEAF, AND COOK. ONCE BOILING, REDUCE THE HEAT AND SIMMER, COVERED, FOR 20-25 MINUTES, UNTIL ALL THE LIQUID IS ABSORBED.
5. REMOVE THE BAY LEAF. TURN OFF THE HEAT AND LET THE RICE COOL FOR AT LEAST 10 MINUTES.
6. PREHEAT THE OVEN TO 350°F (180°C).
7. ADD THE GREEN ONIONS AND BASIL TO THE COOLED RICE AND STIR WELL TO COMBINE.
8. FILL THE TOMATOES WITH THE COOKED RICE MIXTURE. PLACE THE STUFFED TOMATOES

ON THE BAKING DISH AND PLACE THE CUT TOP ON EACH TOMATO. SLIGHTLY COVER THE PAN WITH ALUMINUM FOIL.

9.	BAKE THE TOMATOES IN THE OVEN FOR 20 MINUTES.

10.	REMOVE THE FOIL, DRIZZLE THE TOMATOES WITH THE REMAINING WINE, AND LET THEM BAKE FOR ANOTHER 10 MINUTES. LET THE DISH STAND FOR 5 MINUTES BEFORE SERVING.

Salads
Greek Bulgur Salad

FRESH CUCUMBER AND CHERRY TOMATOES GIVE THIS
HEALTHY DISH A BEAUTIFUL COLOR - IT'S ALSO FULL
OF FIBER AND VITAMIN C.

PREPARATION TIME 35 MINUTES
COOKING TIME 0 MINUTE
SERVES: 4

INGREDIENTS:
3 CUPS BOILING WATER
1 CUP BULGUR
2 TBSP FRESH LEMON JUICE
1 TBSP OLIVE OIL
1 SMALL GARLIC CLOVE, MINCED
½ TBSP SALT
⅛ TSP FRESHLY GROUND PEPPER
¾ CUP FRESH MINT, CHOPPED
2 CUPS CHERRY TOMATOES, HALVED
1 SMALL CUCUMBER, PEELED, SEEDED AND CUT
4 LARGE ROMAINE LETTUCE LEAVES

DIRECTIONS:

1. PLACE THE BULGUR IN A LARGE BOWL, POUR IN 3 CUPS OF BOILING WATER AND IT LET STAND UNTIL THE BULGUR IS TENDER, FOR ABOUT 30 MINUTES.
2. USING A FINE-MESH SIEVE, DRAIN THE BULGUR AND PLACE BACK INTO THE BOWL.
3. ADD THE CUCUMBER, TOMATOES AND CHOPPED MINT TO THE BULGUR. STIR WELL THEN ADD THE OLIVE OIL, LEMON JUICE AND GARLIC. SEASON WITH SALT AND PEPPER. MIX WELL TO COMBINE.
4. PLACE THE LETTUCE LEAVES ONTO SERVING PLATES. SPOON THE SALAD ONTO THE LETTUCE AND SERVE. THIS SALAD IS GREAT SERVED WITH TOASTED PITA BREAD.

VEGAN GREEK QUINOA SALAD

THIS IS A VERY SIMPLE AUTHENTIC GREEK DISH. ADD SOME FRESHLY SQUEEZED LEMON JUICE TO THIS SALAD TO COMPLETE THE TASTE.

PREPARATION TIME 10 MINUTES
COOKING TIME 25 MINUTES
SERVES: 8-10

INGREDIENTS:
1½ CUPS QUINOA
3 CUPS WATER
½ CUP KALAMATA OLIVES, CUT
⅓ CUP PINE NUTS
½ CUP FRESH BASIL, COARSELY CHOPPED
1 CUP FRESH SPINACH, COARSELY CHOPPED
½ CUP FRESH PARSLEY, CHOPPED
½ CUP FRESH CILANTRO, CHOPPED
⅓ CUP SCALLION
⅔ CUP RED ONION
1 CUP TOFU
⅔ CUP WHITE DISTILLED VINEGAR
1 LEMON JUICE AND ZEST
3 GARLIC CLOVES, GRATED
1 TBSP TAHINI

DIRECTIONS:
1.   POUR 3 CUPS OF WATER INTO A LARGE POT AND BRING TO A BOIL OVER A HIGH HEAT.
2.   ADD THE QUINOA, COVER AND SIMMER OVER A MEDIUM-HEAT UNTIL THE QUINOA IS COOKED THROUGH AND ALL THE LIQUID IS ABSORBED. REMOVE FROM THE HEAT, TRANSFER TO A BOWL AND LET IT COOL COMPLETELY.
3.   CUT THE TOFU INTO SMALL CUBES AND PLACE IN A BOWL. ADD HALF OF THE LEMON ZEST AND JUICE, ⅓ CUP VINEGAR AND 1 GRATED GARLIC CLOVE. LET THIS STAND TO MARINATE

FOR ABOUT 20 MINUTES.

4.   IN A LARGE SALAD BOWL, COMBINE THE CHOPPED PARSLEY, BASIL, RED ONION, SCALLIONS AND CILANTRO. ADD THE COARSELY CHOPPED SPINACH AND THE CUT KALAMATA OLIVES.

5.   IN A SMALL BOWL, MIX TOGETHER THE REMAINING LEMON JUICE AND ZEST, TAHINI, RESERVED VINEGAR AND GARLIC, AND SET ASIDE.

6.   ADD THE MARINATED TOFU (WITH THE MARINADE) INTO THE BOWL OF CHOPPED HERBS AND VEGETABLES. STIR IN THE COOLED QUINOA AND POUR THE PREPARED DRESSING OVER THE SALAD, TOSS TO COMBINE.

7.   SPRINKLE WITH CHOPPED PINE NUTS AND ENJOY.

Traditional Greek Potato Salad (Patatosalata)

THIS DISH IS A SIMPLE AND HEALTHY COMBINATION OF INGREDIENTS. THE ADDITION OF THE CHOPPED OLIVES ADDS A LOVELY "BITE" TO THIS SALAD. ONCE YOU TRY THIS DISH YOU WILL BE EAGER TO ENJOY IT AS OFTEN AS POSSIBLE.

PREPARATION TIME 5 MINUTES
COOKING TIME 20 MINUTES
SERVES: 6

INGREDIENTS:
2LBS (907G) ROUND RED POTATOES
KOSHER SALT
FRESHLY GROUND BLACK PEPPER, TO TASTE
⅓ CUP EXTRA VIRGIN OLIVE OIL
3 TBSP WHITE WINE VINEGAR
1½ CUPS PITTED KALAMATA OLIVES, ROUGHLY CHOPPED
⅓ CUP RED ONION, FINELY CHOPPED
2 TBSP FLAT-LEAF PARSLEY, CHOPPED

DIRECTIONS:
1.   PLACE THE POTATOES IN A LARGE POT AND COVER WITH WATER. ADD 1 TABLESPOON OF SALT AND SET OVER A MEDIUM-HIGH HEAT TO BOIL.
2.   ONCE BOILING, REDUCE THE HEAT AND SIMMER FOR 12-15 MINUTES UNTIL THE POTATOES ARE TENDER. POUR OFF THE WATER AND COOL FOR 15 MINUTES.
3.   CHOP THE POTATOES INTO ½ INCH CUBES AND TRANSFER TO A LARGE GLASS SALAD BOWL.
4.   COMBINE THE VINEGAR, OLIVE OIL, ONION AND CHOPPED OLIVES IN A SMALL BOWL, AND SEASON WITH SALT AND PEPPER.
5.   POUR THE DRESSING OVER THE CHOPPED

POTATOES, SPRINKLE WITH CHOPPED PARSLEY
AND GENTLY MIX TO COMBINE. THIS SALAD IS
PERFECT SERVED WARM OR AT ROOM
TEMPERATURE.

CUCUMBER SALAD

THIS IS ANOTHER REFRESHING SALAD YOU CAN TRY FOR YOUR FAMILY. IT CONTAINS CUCUMBERS, ONIONS AND FRESH HERBS WHICH MAKES IT VERY HEALTHY AND PROVIDES YOU WITH LOTS OF VITAMINS.
PREPARATION TIME 5 MINUTES
COOKING TIME 0 MINUTE
SERVES: 6

INGREDIENTS:
1 TSP FRESH OREGANO, CHOPPED
½ CUP RED ONION, THINLY SLICED
2 TBSP FRESH DILL, CHOPPED
2 TBSP RED WINE VINEGAR
2 TBSP FRESH MINT, CHOPPED
1½LBS (680G) CUCUMBERS, HALVED AND SEEDED
3 TBSP EXTRA VIRGIN OLIVE OIL
KOSHER SALT, TO TASTE
FRESHLY GROUND BLACK PEPPER, TO TASTE
HANDFUL OF PARSLEY, CHOPPED

DIRECTIONS:
1. SEED THE CUCUMBERS AND CUT EACH CUCUMBER LENGTHWISE INTO 4 PIECES, THEN CHOP THE CUCUMBERS CROSSWISE INTO THIN SLICES. PLACE THE CUCUMBERS IN A LARGE BOWL.
2. ADD THE OREGANO, ONION, DILL, MINT AND VINEGAR. SEASON THE SALAD WITH SALT AND PEPPER, DRIZZLE WITH THE OLIVE OIL, AND MIX TO COMBINE THE FLAVORS.
3. SPRINKLE WITH CHOPPED PARSLEY AND ENJOY.

Cabbage Salad (Lahanosalata)

LAHANOSALATA IS A CLASSIC AND AUTHENTIC GREEK SALAD, MOSTLY PREPARED IN COLD WEATHERS. FENNEL AND CILANTRO SEEDS, AS WELL AS FRESH THYME LEAVES AND LEMON JUICE MAKE THIS SIMPLE SALAD HEALTHY AND FLAVORFUL.

PREPARATION TIME 15 MINUTES
COOKING TIME 0
SERVES: 6

INGREDIENTS:
1 MEDIUM FENNEL BULB, NO STEMS OR FRONDS
1 MEDIUM (2LBS/907G) HEAD OF CABBAGE
⅓ CUP OLIVE OIL
2 TBSP FRESHLY SQUEEZED LEMON JUICE
3 TBSP RED WINE VINEGAR
¼ CUP FRESH THYME LEAVES
1 TSP SALT
½ TSP FRESHLY GROUND PEPPER
2 TSP MUSTARD POWDER
2 TSP FENNEL SEEDS
2 TSP CILANTRO SEEDS
DIRECTIONS:

1.   REMOVE THE CORE FROM THE CABBAGE AND CUT THE CABBAGE AND FENNEL BULB INTO VERY THIN STRIPS. PLACE THE FENNEL INTO A LARGE SALAD BOWL. USING YOUR FINGERS, BREAK UP THE CABBAGE TO SEPARATE THE THIN STRIPS, AND SET ASIDE.

2.   GRIND THE FENNEL SEEDS AND CILANTRO SEEDS IN A MORTAR AND PESTLE UNTIL FINELY GROUND. TRANSFER TO A SMALL BOWL. ADD THE OLIVE OIL, MUSTARD POWDER, FRESHLY SQUEEZED LEMON JUICE AND OLIVE OIL, AND STIR WELL TO COMBINE.

3.   ADD THE MIXTURE TO THE SLICED CABBAGE AND FENNEL, ADD THYME LEAVES AND MIX TO COAT.

4.   LET THE SALAD STAND FOR 5-10 MINUTES SO ALL OF THE FLAVORS ARE COMBINED BEFORE SERVING.

GREEK ORZO SALAD WITH TOMATOES

THIS IS A WONDERFUL PASTA SALAD FULL OF SUMMER FLAVORS. IT IS QUICKLY PREPARED YET PROVIDES YOU WITH AN UNFORGETTABLE EXPERIENCE.

PREPARATION TIME 5 MINUTES
COOK TIME 10 MINUTES
SERVES: 4 – 6

INGREDIENTS:
1 CUP ORZO, UNCOOKED
½ CUP DILL, CHOPPED
3 TBSP EXTRA VIRGIN OLIVE OIL
1 TSP LEMON ZEST (GRATED)
2 CUPS CHERRY TOMATOES (HALVED)
¾ CUP BLACK OLIVES, PREFERABLY KALAMATA, PITTED
AND HALVED
SALT, TO TASTE
GROUND BLACK PEPPER, TO TASTE

DIRECTIONS:
1. PLACE THE PASTA IN A POT OF BOILING SALTED WATER AND COOK UNTIL AL DENTE.
2. MEANWHILE, IN A LARGE SALAD BOWL, COMBINE THE TOMATOES, OLIVES, OIL, DILL AND GRATED LEMON ZEST, AND SEASON WITH ½ TEASPOON EACH OF SALT AND PEPPER.
3. LET THE MIXTURE SIT FOR 10-15 MINUTES.
4. DRAIN THE COOKED ORZO IN A COLANDER AND ADD TO THE BOWL WITH THE TOMATO MIXTURE. MIX WELL TO COAT.

Greek Couscous Salad with Avocado

THIS IS A VERY TASTY AND HEALTHY SALAD RECIPE
WHICH CAN BE MADE IN A SHORT TIME. SO MAKE SURE
YOU HAVE ALL THE INGREDIENTS ON HAND AND
START EXPERIENCING!

PREPARATION TIME 20 MINUTES
COOKING TIME 5 MINUTES
SERVES: 4

INGREDIENTS:
1 CUP WATER
1 CUP COUSCOUS
1½ TBSP OLIVE OIL (GOOD QUALITY)
2 TBSP RED WINE VINEGAR
2 TBSP LEMON (FRESHLY SQUEEZED)
2 DASHES OF DRIED OREGANO
1 HANDFUL TOMATOES, CHOPPED
1 HANDFUL CUCUMBER, CHOPPED
2 SLICES PURPLE ONION, CHOPPED
½ AVOCADO, DICED
1 HANDFUL ARUGULA
SALT, TO TASTE
GROUND BLACK PEPPER, TO TASTE

DIRECTIONS:
1.   ADD 1 CUP WATER TO A MEDIUM SAUCEPAN
AND SET OVER HIGH HEAT. ONCE IT IS BOILING,
STIR IN THE COUSCOUS AND THEN TURN OFF
THE HEAT. LET THE COUSCOUS STAND FOR
ABOUT 5 MINUTES, COVERED.
2.   IN A SMALL CUP COMBINE TOGETHER THE
VINEGAR, OLIVE OIL, OREGANO AND LEMON
AND SET ASIDE.
3.   PLACE THE CHOPPED CUCUMBER,
TOMATOES AND ONION IN A MEDIUM SALAD
BOWL. POUR THE DRESSING OVER THE

VEGETABLES. ADD THE COUSCOUS TO THE BOWL
AND GENTLY MIX TO COMBINE.
4.   ADD A HANDFUL OF ARUGULA TO A
SERVING PLATE, FLAVOR WITH SALT AND
DRIZZLE WITH OLIVE OIL, IF DESIRED. SPOON
THE COUSCOUS SALAD ON THE PLATE. PLACE A
PIECE OF AVOCADO ON TOP OF THE SALAD AND
SERVE.

Greek Vegan Salad

THIS IS A FANTASTIC PLAIN SALAD RECIPE THAT
FEATURES CLASSIC INGREDIENTS FOR A GREEK SALAD.
IT IS QUICK AND EASY TO MAKE, AND VERY
REFRESHING.

PREPARATION TIME 10 MINUTES
COOKING TIME 0 MINUTE
SERVES: 4

INGREDIENTS:
3 CUPS TOMATO, DICED
3 TBSP FRESH DILL, COARSELY CHOPPED
1 TBSP EXTRA VIRGIN OLIVE OIL
1 TBSP FRESH LEMON JUICE
1 TSP OREGANO, DRIED

42

¼ CUP FRESH PARSLEY, COARSELY CHOPPED
6 CUPS ROMAINE LETTUCE, SHREDDED
1 CUP RED ONION, THINLY SLICED
6 (6-INCH) WHOLE WHEAT PITAS, EACH CUT INTO 8 WEDGES
1 TBSP CAPERS
1 19OZ (540G) CAN OF CHICKPEAS, DRAINED AND RINSED
1 CUCUMBER, PEELED AND THINLY SLICED

DIRECTIONS:

1. IN A SMALL CUP MIX TOGETHER THE OLIVE OIL, FRESH DILL, PARSLEY AND OREGANO.
2. IN A LARGE SALAD BOWL COMBINE TOGETHER THE LETTUCE, DRAINED CHICKPEAS, RED ONION, CAPERS, , CUCUMBER AND TOMATOES.
3. POUR THE PREPARED DRESSING OVER THE SALAD, STIR WELL UNTIL BLENDED.
4. SERVE THE SALAD WITH PITA WEDGES.

Soups and stews

Greek Potato Stew

THIS IS A VERY SIMPLE, BUT A VERY TASTY GREEK DISH. THE KALAMATA OLIVES AND GARLIC PROVIDE IT WITH A WONDERFUL FLAVOR. SERVE WITH PLENTY OF GOOD BREAD TO MOP UP THE DELICIOUS JUICES.

PREPARATION TIME 25 MINUTES
COOKING TIME 30 MINUTES
SERVES: 6

INGREDIENTS:
2½LBS (1134G) POTATOES, PEELED AND CUBED
⅓ CUPS OLIVE OIL
2 CLOVES GARLIC, MINCED
¾ CUP WHOLE KALAMATA OLIVES, PITTED
1⅓ CUPS TOMATOES, CHOPPED
1 TSP DRIED OREGANO
SALT, TO TASTE
GROUND BLACK PEPPER, TO TASTE
DIRECTIONS:
1. ADD THE OLIVE OIL TO A LARGE FRYING PAN AND SET OVER A MODERATE HEAT.
2. STIR IN THE CUBED POTATOES AND GARLIC, AND SAUTÉ FOR A FEW MINUTES.
3. ADD THE OLIVES AND COOK FOR 3-4 MINUTES, STIRRING FREQUENTLY.
4. ADD THE CHOPPED TOMATOES AND OREGANO, REDUCE THE HEAT AND SIMMER, COVERED, FOR 25 MINUTES, OR UNTIL THE POTATOES ARE FORK-TENDER.
5. SEASON THE STEW WITH SALT AND PEPPER, AND SERVE IMMEDIATELY.

Fasolada

FASOLADA IS A TRADITIONAL GREEK DISH THAT IS A
FLAVORFUL COMBINATION OF BEANS, TOMATOES,
CARROTS AND VARIOUS HEALTHY SPICES. BEAN
LOVERS WILL APPRECIATE THIS.

PREPARATION TIME 5 MINUTES
COOKING TIME 1 HR 5 MINUTES
SERVES: 4

INGREDIENTS:
1 CUP WHITE KIDNEY BEANS
1 ONION, THINLY SLICED
2 SMALL CARROTS, SLICED
1 STALK CELERY, CHOPPED
1 14.5OZ CAN DICED TOMATOES
1 TBSP TOMATO PASTE
1 TSP DRIED OREGANO
1 TSP DRIED THYME

46

½ CUP OLIVE OIL
2 TBSP FRESH PARSLEY, CHOPPED
SALT, TO TASTE
GROUND BLACK PEPPER, TO TASTE
DIRECTIONS:

1. SOAK THE BEANS IN COLD WATER AND LET THEM STAND OVERNIGHT. SLIGHTLY RINSE AND DRAIN IN A COLANDER.
2. TRANSFER THE BEANS TO A LARGE POT. COVER WITH WATER AND BRING TO A BOIL. AFTER 3-4 MINUTES POUR OFF THE BOILING WATER, ADD 3 CUPS FRESH COLD WATER AND SET OVER A MEDIUM-HIGH HEAT.
3. ONCE THE WATER RETURNS TO THE BOIL STIR IN THE CARROTS, TOMATOES, ONIONS, TOMATO PASTE, THYME, OLIVE OIL, OREGANO AND CELERY, AND SEASON WITH SALT AND PEPPER. LET THE DISH SIMMER OVER LOW HEAT FOR ABOUT AN HOUR UNTIL THE BEANS ARE TENDER. IN THE END, ADD THE CHOPPED PARSLEY, GIVE A STIR AND REMOVE THE SOUP FROM THE HEAT.

Cabbage Soup

THIS IS A GREAT TRADITIONAL DISH FOR COLD SEASONS IN GREECE THE ORDER OF ADDING THE VEGETABLES IS VERY IMPORTANT IN THIS RECIPE AS IT MAKES THIS DISH HEALTHIER AND MORE FLAVORFUL.

PREPARATION TIME 10 MINUTES
COOKING TIME 30 MINUTES
SERVES: 6

INGREDIENTS:

5 CUPS CHOPPED CABBAGE
⅓ CUP OLIVE OIL
½ CUP CHOPPED ONIONS
⅓ CUP CHOPPED GARLIC
2 CUPS CUBED POTATOES
1 CUP CHOPPED CARROTS
1 CUP CHOPPED ZUCCHINI
2 TBSP FRESHLY CHOPPED DILL
2 TSP DRIED CRUSHED THYME
1½ TBSP SALT
1½ TSP FRESHLY GROUND BLACK PEPPER
7 CUPS WATER
3 TBSP FRESHLY SQUEEZED LEMON JUICE

DIRECTIONS:

1. HEAT THE OLIVE OIL IN A LARGE SAUCEPAN OVER A MEDIUM-LOW HEAT. ADD THE ONIONS AND SAUTÉ UNTIL LIGHTLY GOLDEN AND TRANSLUCENT, ABOUT 3-4 MINUTES.
2. STIR IN THE GARLIC AND SAUTÉ FOR ANOTHER MINUTE, UNTIL JUST TENDER. ADD THE THYME, DILL AND SPRINKLE WITH SALT AND PEPPER. LET IT COOK FOR 2-3 MINUTES ON A LOW HEAT.
3. ADD THE CHOPPED CARROTS AND ZUCCHINI, STIR, AND COOK FOR 10-12 MINUTES.
4. STIR IN THE CABBAGE AND COOK FOR A

FURTHER 2-3 MINUTES, UNTIL THE CABBAGE IS ABOUT TO WILT. FOLD IN THE CUBED POTATOES, STIR UNTIL THEY ARE COATED WITH OLIVE OIL, AND COOK FOR 6-7 MINUTES.

5.   POUR IN THE WATER, INCREASE THE HEAT TO MEDIUM-HIGH, AND BRING THE SOUP TO A BOIL. LET THE SOUP COOK FOR 15-18 MINUTES UNTIL THE POTATOES AND CARROTS HAVE SOFTENED.

6.   FINALLY, DRIZZLE THE SOUP WITH LEMON JUICE AND ENJOY. THIS SOUP IS PERFECT SERVED WITH A PIECE OF CRUSTY BREAD.

Manestra (Orzo Soup)

MANESTRA IS AN AUTHENTIC GREEK DISH THAT'S
PERFECT FOR COLD WINTER DAYS. THE FLAVOR IS
WONDERFUL AND IT IS SO SIMPLE TO PREPARE THAT
YOU WILL BE AMAZED AT HOW SUCH A FILLING DISH
CAN BE SO QUICK AND EASY TO MAKE.

PREPARATION TIME 5 MINUTES
COOKING TIME 30 MINUTES
SERVES: 4

INGREDIENTS:
2 CUPS WHOLE, PEELED TOMATOES
1½ CUPS ORZO
⅓ CUP OLIVE OIL
1 CUP ONION, CHOPPED
2 TBSP DRIED, CRUSHED GREEK OREGANO
1 TSP SALT
1 TSP FRESHLY GROUND PEPPER
4 CUPS WATER

DIRECTIONS:
1.   ADD THE OLIVE OIL TO A MEDIUM
SAUCEPAN AND SET OVER A MEDIUM HEAT. ADD
THE ONIONS AND COOK FOR 3-4 MINUTES, UNTIL
LIGHTLY GOLDEN AND TENDER.
2.   STIR IN THE OREGANO, TOMATOES, ORZO
AND SEASON WITH SALT AND PEPPER. COOK FOR
ABOUT 5-6 MINUTES OVER A LOW HEAT.
3.   ADD THE WATER, COVER, AND COOK FOR
20-25 MINUTES. STIR FREQUENTLY TO AVOID
STICKING TO THE BOTTOM OF THE PAN. THIS
SOUP IS PERFECT SERVED WITH CRUSTY BREAD.

Spicy Greek Pumpkin Soup

THIS IS A VERY TASTY AND HEALTHY SOUP, FULL OF
SPICES AND IT IS VERY SIMPLE TO PREPARE. SURE, YOUR
KIDS WILL ADORE IT.
PREPARATION TIME 5 MINUTES
COOKING TIME 40 MINUTES
SERVES: 4

INGREDIENTS:
2LBS (907G) PUMPKIN, PEELED AND SEEDED
2 TSP EXTRA VIRGIN OLIVE OIL
2 LEEKS, TRIMMED AND SLICED
1 GARLIC CLOVE, CRUSHED
1 TSP GINGER, GROUND
1 TSP CUMIN, GROUND
3 CUPS VEGETABLE STOCK OR WATER
SALT, TO TASTE
BLACK PEPPER, TO TASTE
CILANTRO LEAF, CHOPPED
DIRECTIONS:
1.   PEEL THE PUMPKIN AND CUT INTO COARSE
PIECES. ADD THE OIL TO A LARGE SAUCEPAN
AND SET OVER A MEDIUM HEAT.

51

2.   ADD THE LEEKS AND GARLIC, AND COOK UNTIL TENDER.

3.   STIR IN THE CUMIN AND GINGER, AND COOK FOR A FURTHER MINUTE. ADD THE PUMPKIN PIECES, POUR IN THE STOCK/WATER, SPRINKLE WITH SALT AND PEPPER, AND COOK OVER A MODERATE HEAT.

4.   ONCE BOILING, REDUCE THE HEAT TO LOW AND SIMMER FOR 25-30 MINUTES, UNTIL THE PUMPKIN HAS SOFTENED.

5.   TRANSFER THE SOUP TO A BLENDER AND PULSE UNTIL PUREED.

6.   RETURN THE SOUP BACK TO THE SAUCEPAN AND HEAT FOR 1-2 MINUTES. DIVIDE THE SOUP AMONG SERVING BOWLS, SPRINKLE WITH FRESHLY CHOPPED CILANTRO, AND SERVE IMMEDIATELY.

Greek Stew with Green Beans and Potato

THIS IS AN EASY AND TASTY DISH WHICH IS FULL OF HEALTHY VEGETABLES AND HERBS. THE ADDITION OF CHOPPED ONIONS GIVES IT A NICE CRUNCH.

PREPARATION 5 MINUTES
COOKING TIME 30 MINUTES
SERVES: 10
INGREDIENTS:
1 ONION, CHOPPED
1 TBSP OLIVE OIL
1LB GREEN BEANS, CUT
1 28OZ CAN WHOLE PLUM TOMATOES, WITH JUICE
2 ZUCCHINIS, CUT INTO HALF MOONS
1 LARGE POTATO, PEELED AND CUT INTO CUBES
¼ CUP WHITE WINE
GARLIC, CAYENNE, OREGANO AND THYME, TO TASTE

SALT, TO TASTE
BLACK PEPPER, TO TASTE
FRESHLY CHOPPED PARSLEY

DIRECTIONS:

1.   ADD THE OLIVE OIL TO A LARGE SAUCEPAN AND SET OVER A MEDIUM HEAT. ADD THE ONION AND COOK FOR 3-4 MINUTES, UNTIL LIGHTLY GOLDEN AND TENDER.

2.   ADD THE GREEN BEANS, STIR, AND COOK FOR ABOUT 5 MINUTES. STIR IN THE CHOPPED ZUCCHINI, POTATO, TOMATOES AND GARLIC, WHITE WINE AND SEASON WITH THE GARLIC, CAYENNE, OREGANO, THYME, SALT AND PEPPER.

3.   ONCE THE STEW BEGINS TO BOIL, REDUCE THE HEAT AND SIMMER, COVERED, FOR ABOUT 20 MINUTES UNTIL THE POTATOES HAVE SOFTENED.

4.   LADLE THE STEW INTO A SERVING BOWL, SPRINKLE WITH FRESH PARSLEY AND SERVE WITH TOASTED BREAD.

Fasolakia (Green Bean Stew)

THIS IS NOT A SIMPLE RECIPE TO MAKE, BUT IT IS
DEFINITELY A WORTHWHILE RECIPE. FASOLAKIA IS
ONE OF THE MASTERPIECES OF THE GREEK CUISINE. IT
IS THE PERFECT DISH TO IMPRESS YOUR GUESTS.

PREPARATION TIME 15 MINUTES
COOKING TIME 1 HR 15 MINUTES
SERVES: 6 - 8
INGREDIENTS:
2.2LBS (1KG) FRESH GREEN BEANS, TRIMMED
½ CUP OLIVE OIL
2 ONIONS, PEELED AND GRATED
4 CLOVES OF GARLIC, MINCED
8 ROMA TOMATOES, PEELED AND CHOPPED
2 TBSP FRESH PARSLEY, FINELY CHOPPED
½ CUP WATER
SALT, TO TASTE
BLACK PEPPER, TO TASTE
DIRECTIONS:
1. WASH THE BEANS UNDER COLD WATER.
DRAIN AND REMOVE THE ENDS.
2. ADD THE OLIVE OIL TO A LARGE GRIDDLE
AND SET OVER A MODERATE HEAT. ADD THE
ONIONS AND GARLIC, AND SAUTÉ FOR 3-4
MINUTES, UNTIL LIGHTLY GOLDEN AND
FRAGRANT.
3. ADD THE TRIMMED BEANS AND STIR FRY
FOR 1-2 MINUTES. STIR IN THE TOMATOES, ADD
THE WATER AND SEASON WITH SALT AND
PEPPER.
4. PUT THE LID ON AND SIMMER OVER A LOW
HEAT FOR 60-80 MINUTES, UNTIL THE BEANS ARE
CRISP-TENDER.
5. FINALLY, STIR IN THE PARSLEY, AND SIMMER
FOR A FURTHER 5-8 MINUTES, UNCOVERED,

UNTIL THE TOMATO SAUCE HAS THICKENED.
6.   SERVE IMMEDIATELY.

Greek Chickpeas with Spinach
The combination of spinach and lemon juice is fantastic. Give a try and this stew will become your favorite.

PREPARATION TIME 20 MINUTES
COOKING TIME 1HR 20 MINUTES
SERVES: 6 - 8

INGREDIENTS:
9OZ (250G) CHICKPEAS
2.2LBS (1KG) FRESH SPINACH, ROUGHLY CHOPPED
1 ONION WHOLE
1 LARGE RED PEPPER, DICED
2 CHILI PEPPERS, FINELY CHOPPED
2 TOMATOES, SKINNED AND DICED
1 BUNCH SPRING ONIONS, FINELY CHOPPED
4 TBSP WILD FENNEL, FINELY CHOPPED
2 TBSP PARSLEY, CHOPPED
1 TSP CUMIN POWDER
1 TSP PAPRIKA
1 TBSP LEMON JUICE
½ CUP OLIVE OIL
SALT, TO TASTE
GROUND BLACK PEPPER, TO TASTE

DIRECTIONS:
1. PLACE THE CHICKPEAS IN A POT OF COLD WATER AND LET THEM STAND OVERNIGHT.
2. ADD A WHOLE ONION TO THE CHICKPEAS AND BRING TO THE BOIL. ONCE BOILING POUR OFF THE WATER, ADD FRESH BOILING WATER, AND COOK FOR ABOUT AN HOUR OR MORE, UNTIL THE CHICKPEAS HAVE SOFTENED.
3. TRANSFER TO A COLANDER, DRAIN AND SET ASIDE.
4. ADD THE OIL TO A LARGE SAUCEPAN AND SET OVER A MEDIUM-HIGH HEAT. ADD THE RED

56

PEPPER, SPRING ONIONS AND CHILI PEPPERS, AND COOK FOR 3-4 MINUTES.

5. STIR IN THE TOMATOES AND ADD THE PAPRIKA AND CUMIN.

6. COVER THE SAUCEPAN AND SIMMER FOR 4-5 MINUTES. STIR IN THE CHICKPEAS, SPINACH AND FENNEL, SEASON WITH SALT, STIR, AND SIMMER FOR 10-12 MINUTES, UNCOVERED.

7. STIR IN THE LEMON JUICE, SPRINKLE WITH PEPPER AND CHOPPED PARSLEY. LET THE DISH STAND FOR 5 MINUTES BEFORE SERVING.

Pureed Split Pea Soup

MOST OF US USUALLY HAVE A HARD TIME PERSUADING OUR KIDS TO EAT A SPOON OF SOUP. BE SURE, KIDS WILL ASK YOU FOR MORE OF THIS DELICIOUS AND HEALTHY SOUP.

PREPARATION TIME 10 MINUTES
COOKING TIME 1 HR 20 MINUTES
SERVES: 6 - 8

INGREDIENTS:
1LB (454G) SPLIT PEAS

58

2 LARGE VEGETABLE BOUILLON CUBES
1 LARGE CARROT, CHOPPED
2 STALKS OF CELERY WITH LEAVES, CHOPPED
½ BUNCH OF FRESH PARSLEY, CHOPPED
1 BAY LEAF
⅓ CUP OF OLIVE OIL
SEA SALT, TO TASTE
FRESHLY GROUND PEPPER, TO TASTE
1 TSP DRIED THYME
7-8 CUPS OF WATER

DIRECTIONS:

1. RINSE THE PEAS UNDER COLD WATER AND DRAIN IN A COLANDER. TRANSFER TO A LARGE POT OF COLD WATER AND LET THE PEAS STAND FOR 6-8 HOURS, OR OVERNIGHT.

2. POUR OFF THE WATER AND SLIGHTLY RINSE THE PEAS. ADD THE BOUILLON CUBES, OLIVE OIL, CHOPPED CARROTS, CHOPPED PARSLEY, THYME, BAY LEAF AND CELERY TO THE POT. POUR IN THE WATER, SEASON WITH SALT AND PEPPER, AND BRING THE POT TO A BOIL OVER A MEDIUM–HIGH HEAT.

3. REDUCE THE HEAT, COVER AND SIMMER FOR ABOUT 2 HOURS, STIRRING OCCASIONALLY TO AVOID ANY STICKING TO THE BOTTOM OF THE POT. TASTE THE SOUP AND WHEN YOU SEE THAT THE PEAS ARE TENDER, AND THE SOUP HAS THICKENED ENOUGH, REMOVE THE POT FROM THE HEAT. MAKE SURE THAT YOU DO NOT OVERCOOK THE SOUP.

4. LET THE SOUP COOL FOR 8-10 MINUTES. DISCARD THE BAY LEAF.

5. TRANSFER THE SOUP TO A BLENDER AND PULSE UNTIL PUREED. LADLE THE SOUP INTO SERVING BOWLS AND ENJOY!

Greek Mains
Orzo with Zucchini

THE THREE MOST POPULAR FLAVORS OF GREECE ARE
INCORPORATED INTO THIS RECIPE: GARLIC, OREGANO
AND LEMON. COMBINE THESE WITH THE ORZO,
SQUASH AND A SPLASH OF WHITE WINE AND I PROMISE
YOU WILL CREATE AN UNFORGETTABLE EXPERIENCE.

PREPARATION TIME 10 MINUTES
COOKING TIME 25 MINUTES
SERVES: 6

INGREDIENTS:
2 CUPS ORZO, UNCOOKED
3-4 MEDIUM ZUCCHINI OR YELLOW SQUASH
½ SWEET ONION, CHOPPED
½ CUP OLIVE OIL
½ CUP WHITE WINE
1 TSP SALT
1 TSP FRESHLY GROUND PEPPER
2 TBSP DRIED OREGANO
2 TBSP FRESHLY SQUEEZED LEMON JUICE
4 CUPS VEGETABLE STOCK
2 CUPS WATER

DIRECTIONS:
1.   ADD 2 CUPS OF WATER AND 4 CUPS OF
VEGETABLE STOCK TO A LARGE POT AND SET
OVER A MEDIUM-HIGH HEAT. STIR IN THE ORZO
AND LET IT COOK FOR ABOUT 10 MINUTES, UNTIL
JUST TENDER.
2.   DRAIN WELL, DRIZZLE WITH 1 TEASPOON
OF OLIVE OIL AND SET ASIDE.
3.   ADD THE REMAINING OLIVE OIL TO A
MEDIUM SKILLET AND SET OVER A LOW HEAT.
ADD THE CHOPPED ONIONS, ZUCCHINI AND

COOK, STIRRING FREQUENTLY, UNTIL THE
ONIONS ARE SLIGHTLY GOLDEN AND
TRANSLUCENT.

4.   ADD THE WHITE WINE AND OREGANO, AND
SPRINKLE WITH SALT AND GROUND PEPPER. STIR
WELL TO COMBINE. CONTINUE COOKING FOR AN
ADDITIONAL 10 MINUTES.

5.   STIR IN THE ORZO. AFTER 1-2 MINUTES ADD
THE LEMON JUICE, COVER AND COOK FOR A
FURTHER 10 MINUTES.

6.   SERVE THE ORZO DISH IMMEDIATELY, OR
AT ROOM TEMPERATURE.

SPANAKORIZO (SPINACH AND RICE)

SPINACH IS A GREAT PROPHYLACTIC METHOD FOR THE PREVENTION OF CANCER, CARDIOVASCULAR DEFICIENCY AND THE DEGENERATION OF THE IMMUNE AND NEUROLOGICAL SYSTEMS. THIS DISH CAN EASILY BE INCORPORATED INTO YOUR HEALTHY LIFESTYLE AND, ONCE YOU TRY IT, YOU WILL TURN TO IT AGAIN AND AGAIN.

PREPARATION 5 MINUTES
COOKING TIME 45
SERVES: 4 - 6

INGREDIENTS:
2-3LBS FRESH SPINACH, RINSED AND CHOPPED
¼ CUP OLIVE OIL
1 CUP ONION, CHOPPED
⅓ CUP GARLIC, CHOPPED
¼ CUP FRESHLY CHOPPED DILL OR FRESHLY CHOPPED MINT
1 TABLESPOON DRIED GREEK OREGANO
1 CUP WHITE RICE (MEDIUM GRAIN)
3 CUPS WATER
1½ TSP SALT, TO TASTE
1 TSP FRESHLY GROUND BLACK PEPPER, TO TASTE
½ CUP TOMATO PASTE DISSOLVED IN ½ CUP WARM WATER (OPTIONAL)

DIRECTIONS:
1.   HEAT THE OLIVE OIL IN A LARGE NONSTICK SAUCEPAN OVER A LOW HEAT. ADD THE ONIONS AND GARLIC, AND COOK FOR A FEW MINUTES UNTIL TENDER.
2.   STIR IN THE OREGANO AND DILL/MINT, AND SEASON WITH SALT AND PEPPER. STIR WITH A WOODEN SPATULA TO COMBINE WELL.
3.   DISSOLVE THE TOMATO PASTE IN ½ CUP OF WARM WATER AND ADD TO THE POT.
4.   STIR IN THE RICE AND CONTINUE COOKING

FOR A FURTHER 5 MINUTES. STIR OCCASIONALLY TO PREVENT STICKING ON THE BOTTOM. IF YOU NOTICE THE RICE BEGINS TO STICK TO THE BOTTOM SLIGHTLY REDUCE THE HEAT.

5.   ADD THE SPINACH, POUR IN 3 CUPS OF WATER, STIR, AND BRING THE MIXTURE TO A BOIL.

6.   ONCE IT IS BOILING, REDUCE THE HEAT AND SIMMER, COVERED, FOR ABOUT 30 MINUTES, OR UNTIL THE RICE IS TENDER.

7.   REMOVE THE SAUCEPAN FROM THE HEAT AND LET IT STAND, COVERED, FOR 10-15 MINUTES BEFORE SERVING.

Greek Vegetables

THIS IS A WONDERFUL WAY TO USE FRESH TOMATOES AND CUCUMBERS FROM YOUR GARDEN. THIS DISH IS A GREAT COMBINATION OF VEGETABLE FLAVORS, AND IT CONTAINS A WHOLE ARSENAL OF VITAMINS AND NUTRIENTS.

PREPARATION TIME10 MINUTES
COOKING TIME 35 MINUTES
SERVES: 6

INGREDIENTS:
1 CLOVE GARLIC, MINCED
1 TSP DRIED OREGANO
SALT, TO TASTE
GROUND BLACK PEPPER, TO TASTE
6 TBSP EXTRA VIRGIN OLIVE OIL
8 RED POTATOES, CUT INTO QUARTERS
10 CRIMINI MUSHROOMS, QUARTERED
1 LARGE ZUCCHINI, CUT IN HALF LENGTHWISE, THEN CUT INTO MOONS

DIRECTIONS:
1.   HEAT THE OLIVE OIL IN A LARGE SKILLET OVER A MEDIUM HEAT. ADD THE OREGANO, GARLIC, SALT AND GROUND BLACK PEPPER, AND SAUTÉ FOR A MINUTE UNTIL FRAGRANT.
2.   STIR IN THE MUSHROOMS, POTATOES AND ZUCCHINI.
3.   COVER THE SKILLET AND SAUTÉ THE VEGETABLES OVER A MEDIUM TO HIGH HEAT FOR 5-6 MINUTES.
4.   UNCOVER, REDUCE THE HEAT TO MEDIUM-LOW, AND COOK, STIRRING FREQUENTLY, UNTIL THE POTATOES HAVE SOFTENED AND ARE SLIGHTLY GOLDEN, FOR ABOUT 12-15 MINUTES.

Dolmades (Stuffed Grape Leaves)

PREPARATION TIME 15 MINUTES 50-60 MINUTES
COOKING TIME 45 MINUTES
MAKES: 50 DOLMADES

INGREDIENTS:
1 16OZ (454G) BOTTLE OF GRAPE LEAVES, DRAINED AND
UNROLLED
¾ CUP EXTRA-VIRGIN OLIVE OIL
3 CLOVES GARLIC, MINCED
2 SCALLIONS, MINCED
1 LARGE YELLOW ONION, MINCED
⅔ CUP LONG-GRAIN RICE
KOSHER SALT, TO TASTE
FRESHLY GROUND BLACK PEPPER, TO TASTE
3 TBSP FRESH DILL, MINCED
½ CUP FRESH LEMON JUICE
DIRECTIONS:

1.   PLACE THE GRAPE LEAVES IN A 5-QT. POT
OF BOILING WATER AND COOK FOR 1-2 MINUTES
OVER A MODERATE HEAT. GENTLY DRAIN, STEM

THE LEAVES AND SET ASIDE.

2.   POUR ½ CUP OIL INTO A LARGE FRYING PAN AND SET OVER A MEDIUM-HIGH HEAT.

3.   ADD THE ONIONS, SCALLIONS AND GARLIC, AND COOK UNTIL TENDER, STIRRING FREQUENTLY, FOR ABOUT 3-5 MINUTES. STIR IN THE RICE AND STIR-FRY FOR 2- 3 MINUTES UNTIL TOASTED.

4.   POUR IN 1¾ CUPS OF WATER, SPRINKLE WITH SALT AND PEPPER, AND COOK COVERED, STIRRING FROM TIME TO TIME, FOR A FURTHER 15 MINUTES, OR UNTIL ALL THE LIQUID HAS BEEN ABSORBED.

5.   ADD THE DILL, STIR, AND REMOVE THE RICE FROM THE HEAT.

6.   PLACE 4-5 GRAPE LEAVES ON THE BOTTOM OF THE POT.

7.   TO START ROLLING THE DOLMADES: PLACE 2 TEASPOONS OF THE RICE MIXTURE IN THE CENTER OF EACH LEAF AND FOLD THE LEAF OVER THE RICE. THEN FOLD THE LEFT AND RIGHT EDGES OVER THE TOP, AND GENTLY ROLL TO GET A SMALL CYLINDER. PLACE THE FOLDED DOLMADES IN THE POT, SEAM SIDE DOWN. REPEAT THIS UNTIL ALL THE FILLING AND GRAPE LEAVES HAVE BEEN USED.

8.   IN A SMALL BOWL, MIX TOGETHER THE LEMON JUICE, REMAINING OIL AND 1 CUP OF WATER, AND POUR OVER THE STUFFED LEAVES. PUT A SMALL PLATE OVER THE DOLMADES TO ENSURE THEY REMAIN SUBMERGED, AND PUT THE POT OVER A MEDIUM HEAT. ONCE IT BEGINS TO BOIL, REDUCE THE HEAT AND SIMMER UNTIL THE RICE IS COOKED THROUGH, FOR ABOUT 18- 20 MINUTES.

9.   PLACE THE COOKED DOLMADES ONTO A SERVING PLATTER, ADD SOME COOKING LIQUID OVER THE TOP, AND SERVE. THIS DISH CAN BE

ALSO SERVED AT ROOM TEMPERATURE.

Greek Vegan pasta

MOST OF US ARE FOND OF PASTA, BUT FEW OF US KNOW HOW TO COMBINE IT WITH BASIL, OREGANO AND GARLIC. WHILE TOMATOES ARE A USUAL DRESSING FOR PASTA, THE REST OF THE INGREDIENTS WILL SURPASS ALL YOUR EXPECTATIONS.

PREPARATION TIME 10 MINUTES
COOKING TIME 1 HR 20 MINUTES

SERVES: 4 - 6

INGREDIENTS:
1LB (454G) RIGATONI OR PENNE PASTA
2 TBSP BREAD CRUMBS
1 MEDIUM ONION, THINLY CHOPPED
2 GARLIC CLOVES, MINCED
1½ CUPS HOMEMADE OR CANNED TOMATO SAUCE, OR CRUSHED TOMATOES
1 CUP RED LENTILS
1½ CUPS VEGETABLE STOCK
1 TSP SALT
½ TSP BLACK PEPPER
1 TSP OREGANO
2 TBSP FRESH BASIL, CHOPPED
2 TBSP FRESH PARSLEY, CHOPPED

BÉCHAMEL
4OZ (113G) RAW CASHEWS
3 TBSP SUNFLOWER SEEDS
2 TBSP NUTRITIONAL YEAST
4 CUPS OF WATER
5 TBSP ALL PURPOSE FLOUR
5 TBSP OLIVE OIL OR VEGAN MARGARINE
1 TSP SALT
1 TSP NUTMEG, FRESHLY GRATED
1 TSP BLACK PEPPER, FRESHLY GROUND

DIRECTIONS:

1. ADD ¼ CUP OF WATER TO A MEDIUM SAUCEPAN AND SET OVER A MEDIUM HEAT. STIR IN THE GARLIC AND ONION, AND COOK UNTIL TENDER, FOR ABOUT 5 MINUTES.
2. ADD THE LENTILS, TOMATO SAUCE, VEGETABLE STOCK, OREGANO AND BASIL. SEASON WITH SALT AND PEPPER AND COOK FOR 20-22 MINUTES.
3. STIR IN THE PARSLEY AND CONTINUE COOKING FOR A FURTHER 3-4 MINUTES. ADD SOME WATER, IF NEEDED.
4. COOK THE PASTA IN A POT OF SALTED BOILING WATER UNTIL AL DENTE. DRAIN IN A COLANDER AND SET ASIDE. GENTLY COAT A BAKING DISH WITH OIL AND SPRINKLE WITH BREAD CRUMBS.
5. TRANSFER THE PASTA TO THE BAKING DISH AND TOP WITH THE LENTIL SAUCE.
6. PREHEAT THE OVEN TO 350°F (180°C).
7. TO MAKE THE BÉCHAMEL, PLACE THE SUNFLOWER SEEDS, CASHEW NUTS, YEAST, WATER, NUTMEG, SALT AND PEPPER INTO A BLENDER AND PULSE FOR 2-3 MINUTES.
8. TO MAKE THE ROUX, ADD THE FLOUR TO 5 TABLESPOONS OF HEATED OIL AND STIR-FRY OVER A MODERATE HEAT.
9. ADD THE CASHEW MIXTURE TO THE ROUX AND STIR FREQUENTLY. COOK THE MIXTURE FOR 5-6 MINUTES, UNTIL THE SAUCE HAS THICKENED.
10. TOP THE LENTIL MIXTURE WITH THE CASHEW BÉCHAMEL, AND SPRINKLE WITH BREADCRUMBS.
11. BAKE IN THE OVEN FOR 40 MINUTES, UNTIL GOLDEN BROWN AND FRAGRANT. SERVE HOT.

Braised Eggplant with Potatoes

THIS RECIPE INCLUDES THE CLASSIC GREEK TASTES: TOMATOES, ONIONS, POTATOES, EGGPLANT, HERBS AND OLIVE OIL. GIVE THIS A TRY AND ENJOY!

PREPARATION TIME15 MINUTES
COOKING TIME 50 MINUTES
SERVES: 4

INGREDIENTS:

1LB (454G) EGGPLANT, CUT IN EGG-SIZED CHUNKS (NOT PEELED)
2LBS (907G) POTATOES, PEELED AND CUT
3 MEDIUM ONIONS, CHOPPED
1 BUNCH OF FRESH PARSLEY, CHOPPED
1½LBS (680G) FRESH TOMATOES, PULPED
OLIVE OIL
1½ CUPS OF WATER
1 TSP SALT
4 TBSP OF FLOUR

DIRECTIONS:

1. PLACE THE EGGPLANT PIECES IN A POT OF COLD WATER AND LET IT STAND FOR 30 MINUTES.
2. PLACE THE ONION, TOMATOES, ½ CUP OF OLIVE OIL, PARSLEY, 1¼ CUPS OF WATER AND ½ TEASPOON OF SALT INTO A MEDIUM SAUCEPAN, AND SET OVER A MEDIUM-HIGH HEAT.
3. ONCE BOILING, COVER AND REDUCE THE HEAT TO MEDIUM. COOK FOR 15 MINUTES. ADD THE POTATOES AND ¼ CUP OF WATER, COVER, AND CONTINUE COOKING UNTIL THE POTATOES ARE FORK TENDER, FOR ABOUT 15-20 MINUTES.
4. REMOVE THE EGGPLANT FROM THE WATER, DRAIN WELL, AND SPRINKLE WITH ½ TEASPOON OF SALT.
5. ADD 4 TABLESPOONS OF OLIVE OIL TO A

LARGE SKILLET AND PLACE OVER A HIGH HEAT.
6.   COAT THE EGGPLANT PIECES WITH FLOUR
AND SAUTÉ UNTIL GOLDEN BROWN ON BOTH
SIDES.
7.   TRANSFER THE EGGPLANT TO A PLATE
LINED WITH PAPER TOWELS TO DRAIN.
8.   ADD THE EGGPLANT TO THE SAUCEPAN OF
VEGETABLE SAUCE AND SIMMER, COVERED, FOR
A FURTHER 10 MINUTES. THIS DISH IS PERFECT
SERVED EITHER HOT OR AT ROOM
TEMPERATURE.

Quinoa Mushroom Pilaf

PILAF HAS HAD THOUSANDS OF FORMS AND HAS EXPERIENCED MILLIONS OF DRESSINGS, TRY THIS ONE TOO. GARLIC, PARSLEY, TOASTED NUTS, MUSHROOMS, BLACK PEPPER, AS WELL AS THE SOUR TASTE OF LEMON PROMISE AN INTERESTING EXPERIENCE.

READY IN 30 MINUTES
SERVES: 4 - 6

INGREDIENTS:
OLIVE OIL
2 CLOVES GARLIC, FINELY CHOPPED
1 MEDIUM YELLOW BELL PEPPER, FINELY DICED
1 MEDIUM GREEN BELL PEPPER, FINELY DICED
2 CUPS MUSHROOMS, SLICED
SEA SALT, TO TASTE
GROUND PEPPER, TO TASTE
2 TBSP FRESH PARSLEY, CHOPPED
1 TSP GREEK SEASONING (MINT, LEMON, BASIL, OREGANO MIX)
2 SCALLIONS (WHITE AND LIGHT GREEN SECTIONS), SLICED
SQUEEZE OF FRESH LEMON JUICE
EXTRA VIRGIN OLIVE OIL, TO TASTE
TOASTED PINE NUTS, FOR SERVING (OPTIONAL)

8. **DIRECTIONS:**
1. THOROUGHLY WASH THE QUINOA AND DRAIN IN A FINE SIEVE. TRANSFER TO A RICE COOKER OR A LARGE SAUCEPAN, ADD TWO CUPS COLD WATER, COVER AND COOK UNTIL ALL THE LIQUID HAS BEEN EVAPORATED.
2. MEANWHILE, ADD THE OIL TO A LARGE FRYING PAN AND SET OVER A MEDIUM HEAT.

72

3. ADD THE PEPPERS AND GARLIC TO THE
PAN AND SAUTÉ, STIRRING FREQUENTLY,
FOR 3-4 MINUTES, UNTIL JUST TENDER.
4. STIR IN THE MUSHROOMS AND SEASON
WITH SEA SALT AND GROUND PEPPER.
SPRINKLE WITH THE GREEK SEASONING
AND STIR WELL TO COMBINE. COOK UNTIL
THE MUSHROOMS HAVE SOFTENED.
5. STIR IN THE QUINOA, AND THEN ADD
THE SLICED SCALLIONS.
6. DRIZZLE THE QUINOA WITH FRESH
LEMON JUICE AND THE EXTRA VIRGIN
OLIVE OIL. GENTLY STIR TO COMBINE.
ADJUST SEASONINGS TO TASTE IF
REQUIRED.
7. SPOON THE QUINOA PILAF ONTO A
SERVING PLATE, GARNISH WITH TOASTED
PINE NUTS AND CHOPPED PARSLEY IF
DESIRE AND ENJOY.
8. THIS DISH CAN BE SERVED HOT, OR IT
CAN BE CHILLED AND SERVED AS A SALAD.

Desserts

Fluffy Blueberry Waffles

MAKING THESE WAFFLES IS A REAL PARTY FOR THE
WHOLE FAMILY. MAKE SURE THE KIDS ARE NOT
AROUND, AS THEY WILL EAT ALL THE WAFFLES BEFORE
YOUR GUESTS ARRIVE! TOP THEM WITH FRESH
STRAWBERRIES, IF DESIRED, AND ENJOY.

PREPARATION TIME 15 MINUTES
COOKING TIME 10 MINUTES
SERVES: 4

INGREDIENTS:
2 CUPS WHOLE WHEAT ALL PURPOSE FLOUR
1 TBSP BAKING POWDER
¼ TSP SALT
⅓ CUP APPLE SAUCE
¼ CUP AGAVE NECTAR
1½ CUPS SOY MILK
1 TBSP OLIVE OIL
½ CUP BLUEBERRIES

9. **DIRECTIONS:**
1. COMBINE THE FLOUR, SALT AND BAKING
POWDER IN A LARGE BOWL. IN A SEPARATE
BOWL WHISK TOGETHER THE SOY MILK, APPLE

SAUCE, OLIVE OIL AND AGAVE NECTAR.
2.   POUR THE MIXTURE OVER THE DRY
INGREDIENTS AND MIX UNTIL INCORPORATED.
LET THE BATTER STAND FOR 15 MINUTES.
3.   ADD THE BLUEBERRIES AND STIR.
4.   POUR THE BATTER INTO THE CENTER OF A
WAFFLE IRON AND BAKE ACCORDING TO THE
MANUFACTURER'S DIRECTIONS. REMOVE THE
WAFFLES FROM THE WAFFLE MAKER USING A
SPATULA.

BOBOTA

PREPARATION TIME 5 MINUTES
COOKING TIME 35 MINUTES
MAKES: 1 LOAF

INGREDIENTS:
2 CUPS CORNMEAL, OR COMBINATION OF
CORNMEAL/CORN FLOUR
¾ CUP WATER AT ROOM TEMPERATURE
½ CUP FRESHLY SQUEEZED ORANGE JUICE
½ TSP CARDAMOMS, GROUND
1 TSP BAKING POWDER
½ TSP BAKING SODA
¼ TSP SALT
⅓ CUP SUGAR
3 TBSP OIL (SESAME, LIGHT OLIVE OR VEGETABLE)
2 TBSP ORANGE ZEST

10. DIRECTIONS:
1.   PREHEAT THE OVEN TO 350°F (175°C).
2.   IN A LARGE BOWL, SIEVE TOGETHER THE
CORNMEAL, BAKING POWDER, SALT, BAKING
SODA AND CARDAMOMS.
3.   IN ANOTHER BOWL, DISSOLVE THE SUGAR
IN THE WATER, STIRRING WITH A SPOON, THEN
ADD THE ORANGE JUICE AND OIL, AND MIX
WELL. POUR THE MIXTURE OVER THE DRY
INGREDIENTS AND MIX UNTIL YOU HAVE A
SMOOTH DOUGH.
4.   ADD THE ORANGE ZEST, SLIGHTLY MIX,
AND PLACE THE DOUGH INTO A BAKING LOAF
PAN.
5.   BAKE IN THE OVEN FOR ABOUT 35 MINUTES,
UNTIL GOLDEN. INSERT A TOOTHPICK INTO THE
CENTER TO CHECK WHEN THE LOAF IS COOKED.
IF IT COMES OUT CLEAN THEN REMOVE FROM
THE OVEN.

FINIKIA / MELOMACARONA

ONE-TWO STEPS AND THESE WONDERFUL SWEET AND
CRUMBLY GREEK COOKIES ARE READY TO BE SERVED.
THEY ARE GOOD IN ANY SHAPE AND FORM AND WILL
CREATE A PLEASANT ATMOSPHERE ALONG WITH A CUP
OF COFFEE OR TEA.

PREPARATION TIME 20 MINUTES
COOKING TIME 25 MINUTES
MAKES: 24 COOKIES

INGREDIENTS:

COOKIES
3½ CUPS OF ALL PURPOSE FLOUR
1 CUP OF VEGETABLE OIL
½ CUP ORANGE JUICE
⅓ CUP SUGAR
1 TSP ORANGE ZEST
½ TSP BAKING POWDER

¼ TSP BAKING SODA
½ TSP CINNAMON

SYRUP
½ CUP HONEY OR AGAVE NECTAR
1 CINNAMON STICK
¼ CUP SUGAR
1 – 1½ CUPS FRESHLY SQUEEZED ORANGE JUICE
½ CUP WATER
1 TBSP ORANGE ZEST

11.   **WALNUTS, PISTACHIOS, CHOPPED, TO GARNISH**

12.

13.   **INGREDIENTS**

1.   MIX TOGETHER THE FLOUR, 1/3 CUP SUGAR, BAKING SODA, BAKING POWDER AND CINNAMON IN A LARGE BOWL AND SET ASIDE.

2.   IN A MEDIUM BOWL, MIX TOGETHER THE SUGAR AND ORANGE JUICE, AND THEN WHISK IN THE VEGETABLE OIL. SET ASIDE.

3.   IN ANOTHER LARGE BOWL, MIX TOGETHER THE WET AND DRY INGREDIENTS BY COMBINING ⅓ OF BOTH INGREDIENTS AT A TIME. YOU WILL FINISH WITH A SMOOTH DOUGH. LET THE DOUGH SIT FOR 15-20 MINUTES.

4.   SHAPE SMALL BALLS FROM THE DOUGH AND THEN SLIGHTLY PAT THE BALLS TO FLATTEN. BAKE THE COOKIES IN A PREHEATED OVEN AT 350 F (175 C) FOR 25-28 MINUTES UNTIL THE EDGES ARE SLIGHTLY GOLDEN BROWN. LET THEM COOL.

5.   MEANWHILE, IN A MEDIUM POT, MIX TOGETHER THE HONEY, SUGAR, ORANGE JUICE, ORANGE ZEST, CINNAMON STICK AND WATER, AND COOK OVER A LOW HEAT FOR ABOUT 10 MINUTES, STIRRING FREQUENTLY.

6.   COAT THE COOKIES WITH THE WARM SYRUP ONCE COOKED. GARNISH WITH CHOPPED WALNUTS/PISTACHIOS AND SERVE.

WHEN YOU READ THE LIST OF INGREDIENTS FOR THIS CAKE YOU CAN APPRECIATE THAT YOU ARE ABOUT TO MAKE AN ABSOLUTELY DELICIOUS DESSERT, ONE THAT IS FULL OF VITAMINS AND PROTEINS. YOU CAN ALSO RELAX WITH THE KNOWLEDGE THAT THIS DISH WILL NOT HARM FOR YOUR DIET! TAKE TIME TO STORE THE CAKE IN THE REFRIGERATOR AND ENJOY IT ON THE NEXT DAY AS WELL.

PREPARATION TIME 40 MINUTES
COOKING TIME 1 HR 40 MINUTES 1HR 15 MINUTES
SERVES: 6

INGREDIENTS:
2 CUPS BAKED, MASHED APRICOTS (10-12 MEDIUM
FRESH APRICOTS)
1 CUP ORANGE JUICE
3 CUPS ALL PURPOSE FLOUR
½ CUP ALMOND FLOUR/MEAL
1½ CUPS SUGAR
2 TSP BAKING POWDER
1 TSP BAKING SODA
¾ TSP SALT
½ CUP VEGETABLE OIL OR VERY LIGHT OLIVE OIL
2 TSP FRESHLY GROUND CARDAMOM (20 PODS)
1 TSP GROUND MAHLEP
1 CUP PISTACHIOS/ALMONDS OR WALNUTS, CHOPPED
(OPTIONAL)

14. DIRECTIONS:

1. PREHEAT OVEN TO 400°F (200°C).
2. HALVE THE FRESH APRICOTS, REMOVING THE PIT. PLACE THEM ONTO A BAKING TRAY, SKIN SIDE DOWN, AND SLIGHTLY DRIZZLE WITH BRANDY OR WATER, IF DESIRED. TRANSFER THE APRICOTS INTO THE PREHEATED OVEN.
3. BAKE FOR 30-35 MINUTES. THEN REMOVE FROM THE OVEN AND COOL. GENTLY PEEL THE APRICOTS AND PUT THEM IN A MEDIUM SIZED BOWL. MASH AND SET ASIDE.
4. COMBINE THE ALMOND FLOUR, ALL PURPOSE FLOUR, BAKING SODA, BAKING POWDER, MAHLEP AND SALT IN A LARGE BOWL AND SET ASIDE.
5. IN A SMALL BOWL, WHISK TOGETHER THE SUGAR AND ORANGE JUICE, AND STIR IN THE CARDAMOM. GRADUALLY WHISK IN THE

VEGETABLE OIL AND MASHED APRICOTS.

6.   ADD THIS MIXTURE TO THE FLOUR MIXTURE AND WHISK TO COMBINE. STIR IN THE NUTS, IF USING.

7.   LINE A BAKING DISH WITH PARCHMENT. POUR THE BATTER INTO THE PREPARED DISH AND SPREAD EVENLY. IF BAKING IN A LOAF PAN, BAKE FOR 75 MINUTES; IF USING A 9×13INCH CAKE PAN, 45 MINUTES IS ENOUGH FOR THIS CAKE.

8.   ONCE THE TOP OF THE CAKE IS GOLDEN BROWN AND A KNIFE INSERTED IN THE CENTER COMES OUT CLEAN, REMOVE IT FROM THE OVEN AND COOL FOR 25-30 MINUTES IN THE BAKING PAN BEFORE SLICING.

9.   SLIGHTLY DUST THE COOKED CAKE WITH POWDERED SUGAR AND ENJOY.

TAHINI WALNUT TASTY COOKIES

PREPARATION TIME 15 MINUTES
COOKING TIME 25 MINUTES
MAKES: 18 COOKIES
INGREDIENTS:

COOKIES
3 CUPS FLOUR
1½ TSP BAKING POWDER
½ TSP SALT
½ CUP TOASTED ALMOND MEAL (FLOUR)
½ TSP CINNAMON
1 TSP GROUND MAHLEP
3 TBSP TAHINI
⅓ CUP SUGAR
1 CUP ORANGE JUICE
¼ CUP BRANDY

FILLING
1½ CUPS CHOPPED WALNUTS
⅓ CUP SUGAR
1 TSP CINNAMON
2 TBSP TAHINI
2 TBSP LEMON JUICE
2 TSP LEMON ZEST

15. **DIRECTIONS:**
1. PREHEAT OVEN TO 350°F (175°C).
2. IN A LARGE MIXING BOWL, MIX TOGETHER THE FLOUR, SALT, BAKING POWDER, ALMOND MEAL, CINNAMON AND MAHLEP, AND SET ASIDE.
3. IN A SEPARATE MEDIUM BOWL, MIX TOGETHER THE BRANDY AND ORANGE JUICE, THEN WHISK IN THE SUGAR AND TAHINI, AND SET ASIDE.
4. ADD THE BRANDY MIXTURE TO THE DRY INGREDIENTS AND MIX WELL TO FORM SMOOTH AND SOFT DOUGH. PLACE THE DOUGH IN THE

REFRIGERATOR, COVERED, UNTIL IT IS NEEDED.

5.   TO START MAKING THE FILLING, PLACE THE SUGAR, CINNAMON, LEMON JUICE AND TAHINI IN A SMALL POT AND SET OVER A VERY LOW HEAT. KEEP STIRRING UNTIL THE MIXTURE RESEMBLES A THICK BROWN PASTE. ADD THE CHOPPED WALNUTS AND LEMON ZEST, AND MIX WELL TO COMBINE.

6.   HALVE THE DOUGH INTO 2 BALLS. COAT THE WORKING SURFACE WITH FLOUR AND ROLL OUT 1 BALL INTO A THIN RECTANGLE.

7.   EVENLY SPOON HALF OF THE WALNUT MIXTURE ON TOP OF THE RECTANGLE, SLIGHTLY PRESSING WITH A SPOON. GENTLY FOLD UP THE ROLLED DOUGH INTO A CYLINDER.

8.   USING A SHARP KNIFE, CUT THE CYLINDER INTO THIN CIRCLES. REPEAT THIS WITH THE SECOND BALL OF DOUGH AND FILLING MIXTURE.

9.   PLACE THE CIRCLES ONTO AN UN-GREASED BAKING DISH AND BAKE IN THE OVEN FOR 20-25 MINUTES. TRANSFER THE COOKIES TO A WIRE RACK TO COOL.

10.   ENJOY.

Peach Barley

BAKED PEACHES MARRY THE BARLEY IN THE BEST POSSIBLE WAY IN THIS RECIPE, WHILE THE CINNAMON ADDS A LOVELY TANG TO THE WHOLE DISH.

PREPARATION 2 HRS
COOKING TIME 45 MINUTES
SERVES: 4 - 6

INGREDIENTS

83

1 CUP BARLEY

3 CUPS WATER

½ TSP SALT

3 TSP HONEY (OR AGAVE)

3 TBSP ORANGE JUICE

½ TSP CINNAMON

½ TSP GROUND CARDAMOM

2 WHOLE(2 CUPS CHOPPED) PEACHES (HALVED, ROASTED)

⅓ CUP FRESHLY CHOPPED MINT

16.   DIRECTIONS:

1.   PREHEAT THE OVEN TO 400°F (200°C). RINSE THE PEACHES UNDER COLD WATER, CUT IN HALF AND REMOVE THE PITS. PLACE THE PEACHES ONTO A BAKING TRAY, CUT SIDE UP.

2.   IN A SMALL CUP, COMBINE EQUAL PARTS OF HONEY/AGAVE AND ORANGE JUICE, AND BRUSH THE MIXTURE OVER THE TOP OF THE PEACHES.

3.   BAKE IN THE OVEN FOR ABOUT 25 MINUTES, UNTIL JUST SOFT. LET THEM COOL FOR A COUPLE OF MINUTES BEFORE GENTLY PEELING THE PEACHES AND CUTTING THEM INTO SMALL PIECES. SET ASIDE.

4.   ADD BARLEY TO A POT OF SALTED WATER AND BRING TO A BOIL. REDUCE THE HEAT TO VERY LOW AND SIMMER 40-45 MINUTES, UNTIL TENDER.

5.   IN A SMALL POT, MIX TOGETHER 3 TABLESPOONS ORANGE JUICE, 3 TABLESPOONS HONEY/AGAVE, CINNAMON AND CARDAMOM, AND PLACE OVER A VERY LOW HEAT FOR A FEW MINUTES UNTIL HEATED. SET ASIDE.

6.   WHEN THE BARLEY IS DONE, PLACE IT IN A LARGE MIXING BOWL. POUR THE HOT HONEY MIXTURE OVER THE BARLEY AND STIR WELL TO COMBINE.

7.   LET THE BARLEY MIXTURE COOL AND STIR IN THE CHOPPED MINT AND CHOPPED PEACHES.

8.   PLACE THE BARLEY MIXTURE IN THE REFRIGERATOR AND REFRIGERATE FOR ABOUT 2 HOURS BEFORE SERVING.
9.   PLACE THE CHILLED MIXTURE INTO SERVING BOWLS, SPRINKLE WITH RAISINS AND ANY TOASTED NUTS, GARNISH WITH FRESH PEACH SLICES AND ENJOY.

Greek Lenten Cake

THE SMELL ALONE OF THIS GREEK TAHINI CAKE, FLAVORED WITH CINNAMON, NUTMEG AND CLOVES IS WORTH THE TIME SPENT IN THE KITCHEN.

PREPARATION TIME 10 MINUTES
COOKING TIME 55 MINUTES
SERVES: 10 - 12

INGREDIENTS:
1 CUP <u>TAHINI</u>
¾ CUP SUGAR
1 ORANGE, GRATED
¾ CUP ORANGE JUICE
2¼ CUPS ALL PURPOSE FLOUR
1 DASH SALT
2½ TSP BAKING POWDER
½ TSP BAKING SODA
1 TSP CINNAMON
½ TSP NUTMEG
½ TSP CLOVE
½ TSP ALLSPICE
½ CUP WALNUTS (BROKEN INTO SMALL PIECES)
½ CUP SULTANA RAISINS
   17.   DIRECTIONS:
   1.   PREHEAT OVEN TO 350ºF (180ºC).
   2.   GENTLY COAT A LOAF PAN WITH OLIVE OIL AND THEN SLIGHTLY DUST WITH FLOUR.
   3.   IN A LARGE BOWL MIX TOGETHER THE

FLOUR, BAKING POWDER, BAKING SODA, CINNAMON, NUTMEG, CLOVE, ALLSPICE AND SEASON WITH SALT.

4.   IN A SEPARATE BOWL, USING A HAND-MIXER, WHIP THE TAHINI, ORANGE ZEST AND SUGAR UNTIL SMOOTH, FOR ABOUT 7-8 MINUTES.

5.   STIR IN THE ORANGE JUICE. GRADUALLY WHISK IN THE FLOUR MIXTURE. ONCE MIXED TOGETHER, ADD THE SULTANA RAISINS AND WALNUTS.

6.   ADD THE BATTER TO THE PREPARED BAKING PAN AND BAKE IN THE OVEN FOR 50-60 MINUTES, OR UNTIL A TOOTHPICK INSERTED IN THE CENTER COMES OUT CLEAN. LET IT COOL AND CUT INTO SQUARES BEFORE SERVING.

VEGAN CHOCOLATE NUT COOKIES

THIS IS REALLY A VERY INTERESTING DELICACY, WHICH MIGHT BECOME ONE OF YOUR FAVORITES FOR TREATING YOUR GUESTS.

PREPARATION TIME 10 MINUTES
COOKING TIME 5-10 MINUTES
MAKES: 36 COOKIES
INGREDIENTS:
⅓ CUP PEANUT BUTTER
2 TBSP CANOLA OIL
1 CUP SUGAR
⅓ CUP SOYMILK
1 TSP PURE VANILLA EXTRACT
1 CUP WHOLE WHEAT FLOUR
½ TSP BAKING SODA
½ TSP SALT
1 CUP FARINA
¼ CUP VEGAN CHOCOLATE CHIPS
¼ CUP CAROB CHIPS
½ CUP CHOPPED WALNUTS OR OTHER NUTS

18. **DIRECTIONS:**

1. PREHEAT OVEN TO 425°F (220°C). COAT A BAKING DISH WITH OIL AND SET ASIDE.
2. IN A LARGE MIXING BOWL, COMBINE THE SOYMILK, SUGAR, PEANUT BUTTER, CANOLA OIL AND VANILLA EXTRACT. MIX WELL UNTIL SMOOTH AND FLUFFY.
3. GRADUALLY WHISK IN THE FLOUR, BAKING SODA, SALT, FARINA, CHOCOLATE AND CAROB CHIPS. FINALLY, FOLD IN THE CHOPPED NUTS/WALNUTS AND MIX WELL UNTIL BLENDED.
4. USING A TEASPOON, DROP COOKIES 2 INCHES APART ON THE PREPARED BAKING SHEET, SLIGHTLY FLATTEN, AND BAKE FOR APPROXIMATELY 5 MINUTES, OR UNTIL THE TOP OF THE COOKIES ARE LIGHTLY BROWN.
5. PLACE ON A WIRE RACK TO COOL.

GREEK HALVA

PREPARATION TIME 15 MINUTES
COOKING TIME 10 MINUTES
MAKES: 18 SERVINGS
INGREDIENTS:
1 CUP OLIVE OIL
2 CUPS GROUND SEMOLINA
2½ CUPS SUGAR (OR LESS)
1 TSP CINNAMON
4 CUPS HOT WATER
1 CUP RAISINS (OPTIONAL) OR 1 CUP NUTS (OPTIONAL)
DIRECTIONS:
1.   ADD THE OLIVE OIL TO A HEAVY CAST SKILLET AND SET OVER A MEDIUM-HIGH HEAT. ADD THE SEMOLINA AND STIR-FRY FOR 3-4 MINUTES UNTIL LIGHTLY GOLDEN.
2.   STIR IN THE SUGAR AND NUTS (IF USING), AND STIR-FRY FOR ANOTHER 3-4 MINUTES.
3.   ONCE THE SEMOLINA BECOMES GOLDEN-BROWN, POUR IN THE HOT WATER.
4.   REDUCE THE HEAT AND KEEP ON STIRRING UNTIL YOU HAVE A THICK MIXTURE. LET IT STAND FOR 10 MINUTES TO COOL.
5.   PLACE THE HALVA INTO A RIMMED ROUND PAN, OR INTO INDIVIDUAL SERVING PLATES, SPRINKLE WITH CINNAMON AND NUTS/RAISINS AND ENJOY!

SPICY BAKED APPLES WITH HONEY SYRUP

WHEN YOU TRY THESE AMAZING APPLES YOU WILL
FEEL LIKE YOU'RE IN HEAVEN! THE SERVING MUST
ALSO BE AS DECENT AS THE DISH ITSELF TO PROVIDE
THE BEST EXPERIENCE FOR THE GUESTS.
PREPARATION TIME 5 MINUTES
COOKING TIME 45 MINUTES
SERVINGS: 6

INGREDIENTS:
4 MEDIUM COOKING APPLES
¼ CUP WALNUTS, CHOPPED (OPTIONAL)
¼ CUP GOLDEN RAISINS
1 TSP HONEY
½ TSP GROUND CINNAMON
¼ TSP GROUND CLOVES
1 CUP WATER
1 CUP HONEY
1 TSP LEMON JUICE
1 CINNAMON STICK
WHIPPED CREAM (OPTIONAL)
DIRECTIONS:

1. PREHEAT THE OVEN TO 375°F (190°C). CAREFULLY CORE THE APPLES, MAKING SURE NOT TO CUT THROUGH THE BOTTOM.
2. IN A MEDIUM BOWL, MIX TOGETHER THE WALNUTS, RAISINS, GROUND CLOVES, CINNAMON AND HONEY.
3. USING A TEASPOON, POUR THIS MIXTURE INTO THE CENTER OF THE APPLES.
4. ARRANGE THE FILLED APPLES IN A BAKING PAN.
5. ADD THE HONEY, WATER, CINNAMON STICK AND LEMON JUICE TO A SMALL POT AND BRING THE MIXTURE TO A BOIL. COOK FOR 1-2 MINUTES, STIRRING CONSTANTLY.
6. DISREGARD THE CINNAMON STICK AND POUR THE HOT SYRUP OVER THE APPLES.
7. TRANSFER THE BAKING PAN TO THE OVEN AND BAKE FOR ABOUT 40 MINUTES. DURING THE BAKING BASTE THE APPLES 3-4 TIMES WITH THE PREPARED SYRUP.
8. ENJOY THE BAKED APPLES WARM OR COLD.
19.

CONCLUSION

WE HOPE YOU HAVE ENJOYED USING THIS COOKBOOK WHICH IS FULL OF CHEF D'OEUVRES OF GREEK COOKING. THE GREEK CUISINE IS REAL HEAVEN FOR GOURMANDS.

I AM SURE YOU HAVE NOTICED THAT THE BASIS OF THE RECIPES IS HEALTHY FOOD, INCLUDING FRESH VEGETABLES, FRUITS, GRAINS, OLIVE OIL, BEANS AND MANY OTHER INGREDIENTS WHICH WILL PROVIDE YOU WITH A VALUABLE ENERGY SUPPLY THAT YOUR BODY NEEDS.

EVERY RECIPE HAS BEEN DEVELOPED WITH THE INTENTION TO MAKE YOUR TIME IN THE KITCHEN

EASY AND ENJOYABLE. WE HAVE PRESENTED TO YOU
SOME OF THE EASIEST, YET HEALTHIEST PREPARATION
METHODS WHICH YOU CAN APPLY TO MAKE YOUR
FOOD BOTH FULFILLING AND DELICIOUS.

HOPEFULLY THIS COOKBOOK WAS ABLE TO HELP YOU
TO VERIFY YOUR MENU IN PREPARING A HEALTHY AND
DELICIOUS GREEK MEAL.